Grandma: some of her ways

Grandma: some of her ways

*Stories by the
Grandchildren of Victorian Women*

As told to
Margaret Bard

The Pentland Press
Edinburgh – Cambridge – Durham – USA

First published in 1998 by
The Pentland Press Ltd
1 Hutton Close
South Church
Bishop Auckland
Durham

ISBN 1-85821-534-X

Typeset by Carnegie Publishing, 18 Maynard St, Preston
Printed and bound by Antony Rowe Ltd, Chippenham

Dedicated to my Grandchildren
Ellen and Sarah Bard

Contents

Illustrations

Foreword

here have been many books written about 'elite' women and 'poor' women of the Victorian age, but few about the 'ordinary' Victorian housewife. My aim was to find out about the lives of such women, starting with my own Grandmothers, whom I remember with clarity and deep affection. Was I alone? Most people I asked were vague, but occasionally there were people who remembered their Grandmother clearly. Photography at that time was in its heyday, the results being almost an art form. Many families have kept these portraits of their Grandmothers carefully. Indeed, the photographs themselves are almost indestructible.

As my enthusiasm grew, I sought out artifacts of the period. I discovered a diary kept by a lady in the middle of the last century.

Who could not warm to the clay pipe smoking Grandma as she sat knitting in her rocking chair, still a force to be reckoned with, or smile at the picture of the Grandmother who was co-driver with her husband in the early motor car, the BEAN?

A few elderly friends declined to have their names acknowledged, fearing that so frank a portrait of their family would disconcert the younger members. It could be viewed as being an indiscretion at the close of their lives.

In an age when 'respectability' and 'keeping up appearances' was the name of the game, I have sought to unravel Grandmother's side of the story and, in so doing, have discovered that there was no such thing as a 'typical' Victorian woman.

Acknowledgements

hose who agreed to be acknowledged by name are: Freddie Axford, Ruth Bailey, Marjorie Barrett, Denise Barton, Norma Bedford, Nina Bishop, Dorothy Bolton, Joyce Boughton, Robin Brown, Mary Chidlow, Lesley Cuthbert, Ray Edmondson, Jean Hammerton, Sybil Harris, Connie Hazell, Mrs Hooper, Betty Jackson, Margaret Laffey, Joan Lewry, Joan Mackay, Peter Moores, Vera Poole, Elizabeth Reader, Ron Rourke, Jean Rushton, June Russell, Margaret Scott, Audrey Smith, Jean Strachan, Sybil Ward and Nellie Wright.

I would also like to acknowledge, with much gratitude, the encouragement and support I received from my family and friends, not forgetting those who chose to remain anonymous.

Margaret Bard

Preface

I grew up listening to family stories. They always fascinated me. My maternal Grandma would recount the memories of her strong-minded husband, whilst my father would often tell of his boyhood in the country of Herefordshire at the turn of the century.

The time for recounting these stories would be at Sunday lunch, when a leisurely break was taken from the hurly burly of the working week. Both my parents worked. No one could stop my father reciting 'Marmion' from start to finish, or stem the flow of his endless tales of my Grandfather's work as a wheelwright and gamekeeper at the Big House.

But it was the stories about my friends' Grandmothers which really fascinated me. What did they do in the household every day? How did they spend their leisure, if they had any? And their strong faith, how did they practise it?

Many accounts have been documented about women from the aristocracy, and many others about those from the poorest classes, but 'ordinary' Victorian wives and mothers have been passed over. I feel that the stories make interesting reading and are a great tribute to the women who had little education but kept a standard and spirit which rarely let them down.

First-hand memories are the best ones, and it is thanks to my friends that I have been able to compile this book.

Tennyson became Poet Laureate after the death of William Wordsworth in 1850. Mrs Beeton produced her cookery book around 1860; Florence Nightingale sought to promote an efficient nursing service; the 1870 Education Act provided elementary education for all children.

More modern dress for ladies was emerging, with the crinoline giving way to the bustle. For 'ordinary' women, 'Sunday Best' was worn only on Sundays, or on rare special occasions such as a wedding or perhaps a railway excursion. Women's clothes represented convenience – and utility. It was the First World War which brought about a still more radical change in the clothes which women wore. No longer were ladies bundled up in layers of clothing; in winter women wore long, full skirts of thick material, maybe serge; colours would be black, brown, navy or dark green. Blouses with high necks were fashionable, cotton in the summer and perhaps flannel in the winter. Costumes were also fashionable. Lace-up or button-up boots, with black or brown stockings, were in vogue. Of course, corsets, fashioned in the manner of armour plating, were worn under all these garments – it seems amazing that any work could be done when wearing them, let alone play! Large fashionable hats needed at least two hatpins to keep them from blowing off. On Mondays, meals took second place to the washing, when clothes were washed in the copper in the corner of the kitchen. Wash day was Monday. The fire had to be laid, maybe on Sunday night, the water being taken from the tap or from the rain barrel in the garden.

Time was heavily structured. The whole street seemed to succumb to order and ritual. 'Ordinary' women, whom this book is about, knew their place in society, and were either happy with the terms or put up with them. Opportunities for working class mothers to escape from a life of domestic routine were rare. Right up to the Second World War, whilst she could take in washing or ironing, could clean other people's houses or let rooms to lodgers, mother's place was 'in the home'.

But it was via the family photographs *en famille* that the Victorians perhaps wished to be remembered. Photographic studios abounded, and their work provided a unique insight into the social history of the period.

Although there were lending libraries in Grandmother's day, they were not a feature of most women's lives. Their reading focused on magazines for women – *Family Friend, Family Treasure, Family Record, Home Thoughts*, the *Home Friend*, the *Home Companion* and the *Home Circle*. The *Sunday at Home* was a family magazine for sabbath reading. Home and family were the circumscribed limits of most working class women's vision.

These magazines, plus chapel or church, encouraged our Grandmothers to live a 'righteous and sober' life, together with the community, which was always watchful of those who failed to keep to the straight and narrow. Women did gossip and were capable of strict judgement on others.

All these factors led a dutiful and submissive daughter, brought up to do her share of the household chores, into being an equally dutiful and submissive wife. She fed her children to the best of her ability, kept them warm and clean and taught them right from wrong, only calling on her husband to back her up with a show of strength from his trouser belt or razor strop, if all else failed. A good wife attended to her husband's needs. A good husband, in turn, gave his wife enough money for housekeeping.

Of course, people often failed to keep to these high standards. Men frequently gambled or drank heavily; both sexes could be involved in illicit and clandestine affairs; the 'liberated' woman was not unknown in Grandmother's circle. Many women worked in factories and did 'men's' jobs in the First World War.

But divorce was uncommon, and most couples kept together, at least outwardly. 'Keeping up appearances' was true in most houses, at whatever cost.

Part One
The Beaded Bag Opened

With cap-framed face and long gaze into the embers
We seated around her knees—
She would dwell on such dead themes, not as one who remembers,
but rather as one who sees.

'One we Knew'
Thomas Hardy

Introduction to Part One

hilst our Grandmothers were busy bringing up their children, making the most of what little spare time they had, attending church or chapel, or not, making the money last until the next pay day, rarely knowing anything about holidays – what was going on in the world outside?

For example, what was happening in the fast expanding town of Bournemouth, Dorset? The Borough grew very rapidly from the beginning of the middle fifties of the nineteenth century to the dawn of the twentieth. The climate was mild; there was plenty of work for the skilled and the unskilled in the developing areas around the heart of the town and in rural districts which were gradually incorporated within its boundaries.

Winton was one such area in 1891. Although there were about 4,000 inhabitants, it was a community in its own right, being separated from Bournemouth's centre by gorse-covered, undeveloped land. By 1898 Winton had become an Urban District; in 1899 the population was 7,249; in 1901 Winton finally became part of Bournemouth.

Some, although not all, of the women whose ways are told in Part One brought up families in Bournemouth. These are their stories . . .

Madam's
Pretty Little Parlour Maid

Mary Ann Carter (1862–1953)

Strictly religious, family orientated, Mary Ann was prepared to move house repeatedly to advance her husband's career.

I loved my Grandma, she was always there for me.

Throughout my childhood, I rarely saw her leave her house in Winton, Bournemouth. She was born in 1862 and was ninety-one when she died. She had a recollection of a soldier returning to her village in Ashperton, Herefordshire, in rags; he had been in the Crimean War. Or it could have been a tale that she heard from her Grandparents regarding Waterloo. Anyway, she often recounted the story of the soldier returning home with the blood oozing out from the laces of his boots. The picture was graphic!

One of six children, my Grandma, Mary Ann Hill, nicknamed Polly, was the eldest girl. She left school at twelve years of age and went into service, the normal occupation for a girl living in rural Herefordshire. Mary Ann's father was a carrier – his horse and cart service operated between Ashperton (where the family lived) and Ledbury, in Herefordshire. Her father carried both people and goods. Her mother was a midwife.

Grandma was known as the lady of the house's 'pretty little parlour maid'. Gran married William Derham Carter, who came from Hinton Admiral, Christchurch. He rode a penny-farthing bicycle from Christchurch to Bournemouth. During their married life, they lived in Bournemouth, Ledbury, Birmingham, Kidderminster and Atherstone, returning to Bournemouth where Grandfather was a Food and Drugs Inspector for the borough. He also left school at twelve, but attended night school after leaving. My Grandparents were surprisingly mobile for the times (many

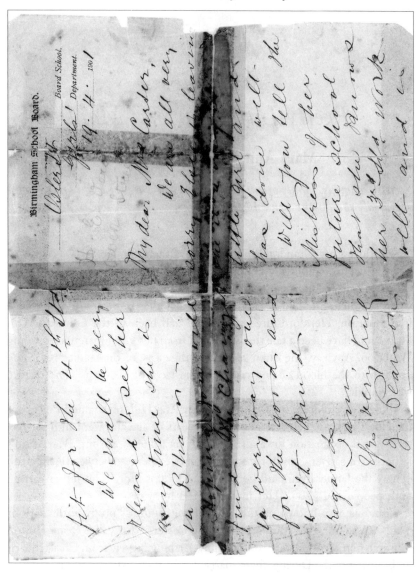

Letter sent to Mary Ann Carter from the schoolmistress

people stayed where they were born), but if one wanted to get on, one had to leave the countryside for work in the towns. Obviously Grandad moved about for promotion; he had begun his working life as a plumber.

To help with the family budget, Grandma, like many other wives in Bournemouth, took in paying guests while her children were growing up.

My mother used to tell of her early courting days in Bournemouth with my father. Mum was introduced to Dad on the top of a tram – Dad was home on leave at the time; he was a First World War soldier. After the introductions, Dad took my mother and her friend, together with his little sister, to the pictures. Mum had intended to walk along the pier but the weather (or Dad) changed her mind. On my mother's first 'date' alone with Dad, Grandad was detailed, by my Grandma, to walk, discreetly, on the other side of the road from the pair. Grandad was not happy with this arrangement, but 'nice' girls needed chaperoning. I don't expect Mum let on about the pictures! My parents were in their late twenties at the time.

My Grandmother (or perhaps my Grandad) did not believe in girls receiving an education after twelve years old, although Gran's sister, my Great Aunt Lizzie, herself successful in business, did – she was of the opinion that when you educate a girl, you educate a family. My mother was the eldest, with two brothers following. The elder boy was sent to Bournemouth Grammar School, the injustice of the action so incensing my mother that she vowed that all her girls would be educated. Fortunately, she had only two, my sister and myself – and my Granny bore the cost of educating my sister. However, my mother did have singing lessons and learnt to play the piano.

Opposite: a letter written to Mary Ann Carter from the school mistress. It reads:

19.4.1901

My Dear Mrs. Carter

We are all very sorry Elsie is leaving. She is a bright little girl and has done well.

Will you tell the mistress of her future school that she knows her 3rd Standard work and is fit for the 4th Standard.

We shall be pleased to see her any time she is in B'ham.

Hoping you will find the change in every way one for the good and with kind regards

I am
Yours very truly

When I was young we lived round the corner from my Grandparents. Sadly, in 1934 my Grandfather died, aged sixty-four years. I was four years old and never again was bounced on trousered knees and had my neck tickled by a moustached face! Grandad was a very generous man, who put the deposits down on the houses for my mother and her brother.

Soon after my Grandfather's death, my Great-Aunt Fanny Hill came to live with Gran. Fanny had been companion to Lady Maclean and felt herself a cut above everyone else. When she left the Maclean family, she was awarded an annuity for life.

Grandma always made my summer dresses with knickers to match, by hand, and a nightdress every Christmas. She made me sets of dolls' clothes also. On school days, my brother, sister and I, separately, would call to see Gran on the way home from Alma Road School. We were inspected for clean nails, a clean handkerchief and tied shoe laces. As I was often minus a handkerchief, Gran would give me one of hers, but as I lost so many, a clean rag was offered and gratefully accepted. When Grandma came to the back door, in answer to our knock, she would be carrying a brown tin containing Bluebird toffees, assorted flavours. We could choose two, one in the mouth and one in the hand. The journey back home would be pleasurable, sucking the sweet and skipping along.

Grandma and Grandad were members of the Plymouth Brethren, the exclusive Brethren, who were very strict and unworldly. No radio or Sunday papers were permitted and few amusements, and they maintained a very narrow outlook on life. However, Gran did take the *News Chronicle* and, daringly, the magazine *Picture Post*. They were great admirers of Queen Victoria and Mr Gladstone, of whom very large photographs adorned the sitting room walls.

The Brethren Meetings were held in a hall over Lansdowne post office in Bournemouth. Men alone led the meetings, and the hymns were always sung unaccompanied.

Before marriage, however, my mother did play her part in the service, on long summer evenings. Grandad would conduct an open-air meeting held at the bottom of the Eastcliff zig-zag, where two of the Brethren would carry a harmonium for my mother to play. The music would attract the attention of the people who were taking the sea air.

Before the last war, during the school holidays, Grandma would some-times take me to the beach, and stay all day. We always sat under

Bournemouth Pier. This was the ritual for the day: I walked to my Gran's house promptly at 10.30. That was the time any pre-arranged activity for the day started. Grandma would be all ready and the picnic basket packed. It contained many banana sandwiches (why, I could never understand for we were never offered than at any other time!), homemade cakes and a flask of tea. We would catch the petrol bus which passed near Gran's house, and alight near the Pleasure Gardens.

But it was Grandma's beachwear which always fascinated me. Without fail, she wore a long black dress, over which she always wore a light shiny black mackintosh – whatever the weather. Her hat was black and so were her shoes. To finish off her beachwear, she brought an umbrella, which was put up immediately we reached the pier and only taken down when the day's outing was over.

Grandma's rigid routine gave me a great sense of security – both my parents worked. Whatever changed at home, nothing changed at Grandma's. For example, on Mondays for the mid-day meal, there was always cold meat, boiled potatoes and mustard, followed by apple dumplings. It was Gran's wash day, and there was not much time for preparing food. On Tuesdays, ironing day, there would be a thick stew. Every day at four o'clock sharp, tea would be prepared in the sitting room, with a dainty white cloth, paper thin brown and white bread, and butter and homemade jam. Before every meal, grace was said either by Grandma or by Great-Aunt Fanny.

Christmas tea was always spent with Grandma. It was one of the very few events in my childhood which all the family did together. Just before four o'clock, we would set off along the deserted roads to tea, where we had Dundee cake, never a Christmas cake. In fact, there was little sign of Christmas celebrations. I used to put it down to Gran's great age but maybe it was her Exclusive Brethren doctrine which did not allow her to celebrate Christmas in the accepted tradition. Then at six o'clock we ambled back to our house and put on the wireless.

Grandma's stories about Grandfather were numerous. At one time, an Alderman who owned a grocery shop in the town had been reported for watering down the vinegar. My Grandfather took the case to court; although many people advised him that 'you don't take an Alderman to court', my Grandfather did and won the case. He always said, 'If a thing is right, it is right, and if it is wrong, then it is wrong.' Grandad now drove an Austin

Seven; it was painted buttercup yellow and black. We were taken out occasionally into the country – what a treat!

On another occasion when there had been many deaths of small babies (in a local area) there was some doubt as to whether the milk was sufficiently nourishing. In those days milk came in a churn and was ladled into the purchaser's jug by the roundsman. Grandfather was suspicious and, very early in the morning, he waited at Winton Banks for the milkman to appear on his rounds. To Grandfather's horror, the milkman carried the milk churn down to the gents' lavatory. He was going to dilute the milk from the water tap! Grandfather took a sample of the milk; the miscreant jumped on his back and tried to spill the evidence. However, he was brought to justice and the babies no longer died from poor quality milk.

The only time my Grandma heard the wireless was when she visited us once a year, while Great-Aunt Fanny was on holiday in Andover with relatives. During her stay, Gran would say, every afternoon at four o'clock, 'Time for Mrs Dale's Diary.' She loved that programme. She disliked the weather forecast and would look up to where the wireless was housed and say, 'There's only one who knows!'

Everything was so ordered, nothing seemed to alter. Till the day Gran died, at home, Queen Victoria looked down on her from the wall in the sitting room, white bonneted and side-viewed. On the wall facing the window in Gran's front bedroom, looking down on the double bed with the thick feather mattress, was a photogravure of Marcus Stone's, entitled, 'Two's company, three's none'. Men in cocked hats and women in Empire line dresses gave the public the nostalgia they had for a mythical pre-industrial Golden Age of lost elegance and leisure.

I always loved that picture and felt so safe when, snug in bed with Grandma, I would glance up to where the couple, obviously very much in love, were seated, behind which a matronly figure stood, ready to depart, or stay!

On one occasion, Gran made me a little outfit of skirt, bolero and lined knickers. With it I wore a shantung blouse and a white angora beret, which my mother had knitted. Gran made the garments out of a red velvet dress which my Great-Aunt Lizzie (Gran's sister) had sent to my mother. After each of my aunt's sales, a round hat box would be delivered to my mother in Bournemouth, from Andover, with dresses and hats which had not sold. It was a red letter day when we received the box. Included one year was this glamorous red velvet dress, quite unsuitable for my mother to wear to the Baptist Chapel, but the material was perfect for me. With Gran's expertise, the dress was cut up and delegated as my Sunday wear.

Back to Aunt Lizzie. She owned a very high-class ladies' wear shop in Andover, and one of the conditions under which she was allowed to trade was that in the window of her shop she was to display only one dress, one hat, one handbag, one pair of gloves and one pair of shoes. Good taste and exclusiveness was essential. Auntie traded under the name 'Madame Pepler'. Her house and shop may have been owned by the Church of England and was called Bishop's Court; it was very grand. When I stayed alone with my aunt and uncle in the school holidays, I slept in a room with rounded walls and a sloping floor. My imagination knew no bounds when I went to bed, but I never saw a ghost or was too afraid with the shadows which my nightlight made on the ceiling, and on the curvy walls.

It must have been my first year at Grammar School when, one day, I decided to tell my school friends about the red velvet knickers. Now, normal wear was strictly navy knickers. The girls dared me to wear the voluminous red underwear under my tunic. Always loving a dare and attention, I came the next day, cartwheeling and handstanding all over the classroom and playground. I still remember the glow the unusual action gave me. My French Great-Grandmother would have been proud of me! Not quite the Can-can, but the best performance that I could achieve.

To return to my memories of my Grandmother. She had a hairpiece, measuring about two inches by three. The hair (Gran's own) was encased in a light hair net. Each evening it was carefully put on the dressing table in a china tray which stood in front of the mirror and was the receptacle for hair pins, hair nets, brooches and other necessary equipment. Now whether Gran had made the hairpiece out of lengths of hair from her comb (which she collected in a small cone-shaped 'tidy' hanging up on one side of the mirror), or from cuttings of her long hair, I do not know, but the hairpiece was a fact of life.

Every morning Gran arose at eight o'clock and washed in the cold, north-facing bathroom in which was a large wash basin, a choice of soap (Lux or coal tar), a bath and a toilet. Here Gran dressed, after washing herself.

But she needed the mirror (there was none in the bathroom) in order to dress her hair. She had a large mirror in her bedroom. The long, wispy grey hair was brushed upwards on to the top of her head and secured with hair pins. Gran had a widow's peak, a V-shaped formation of hair at the front of her forehead. Constant brushing (in the wrong direction) had worn the hair away and there was a baldness there. Now this is where the hairpiece came in. It was a very subtle move on Gran's part, for had I not observed the preparation with my own eyes, from the bed, I would never have known.

Gran remarked one day, out of the blue, that she disliked women who wore red nail varnish. Her next sentence came as rather a shock: 'They look as if they have been skinning rabbits!' Gran could speak with authority, as she had often performed that very task.

Her strong feelings were prompted after seeing her evacuees' mother for the first time. It was during the Second World War and, although Gran was past the age when children should be foistered on to her, she was obliged to give the two children from Southampton room and board, whilst that city was going through the terrible Blitz. Fortunately, their stay was brief.

Not only was the mother a 'fur-coated Jezebel' in Gran's eyes, but an unsuitable one, to boot. The mother left her six-year-old girl with Gran in 'what she stood up in', which was a backless sun-dress and a pair of plimsolls. No luggage! Obviously she had been dressed for a day on Bournemouth sands, not a long time stay. However, Gran soon had Doreen kitted out at her own expense. The boy fared better. He was suitably clad.

This incident was the only introduction Gran had to 'the high life'.

Even towards the end of her long life, Gran was always particular about her personal hygiene. She kept a used lemon on the side of the kitchen sink to be rubbed over her hands after washing up in soda water. She was always nice to be near, and ready to instruct her grandchildren in her ways. I remember on one occasion I was invited to have a strip-wash, having lain on her sofa for hours recovering from a bout of teeth-removal by gas. No allowances were made for the fainthearted!

Lux flakes were used for her washing days – clothes would have needed only the minimal washing as she neared ninety years of age. Yellow bar soap was used to scrub the red tiles on the kitchen floor. From the age of ten, it was my job on a Saturday morning to scrub the kitchen floor. I was rewarded with a sixpence; but I did not like taking it. It was a pleasure to do something for Gran in return for all the things she did for me.

I grew up during the Second World War. I loved to stay with my Gran and Great-Aunt Fanny for the weekend. Well, it was all day Saturday, returning home early on Sunday morning in order to attend Sunday School at 10.15. We children would then troop into the chapel for the 11 o'clock service, being allowed to leave before the sermon for the grown-ups had started, about 11.45. When I had not stayed the weekend with Gran, she would often invite me to Sunday tea. Being an active child, the few suitable books which I was able to read there soon exhausted my attention, and I would retreat to a small back room facing the garden. The sun always came into this room, consequently the blinds were never pulled up. They remained unpulled as the rather lovely deep blue carpet would have faded. This lent an air of mystery to the feel of the room – it was never dark, but my imagination would go into overdrive, especially when I sought the harmonium which was housed in the corner farthest from the door, and begin to pedal away, and play away, starting off with as many hymns as I could play 'off by heart'. I then progressed to the music in a book of chants which Gran possessed, the only music book in the room. How this book found its way into Gran's house is anyone's guess!

I was transported into a world of my own. I knew that Grandma and Great-Aunt Fanny weren't at all interested in my playing. I was just amusing myself, and not worrying them – not asking for dolls' clothes to be made next week, or a more exciting book to read – or any book to read! Of course, a request to play ball on a Sunday, outside, would be absolutely forbidden.

Quietly playing dull music for too long was against my nature. I needed to liven things up! Daringly, I would start to play the songs of the Forties – 'Sentimental Journey' and 'In the Mood' to name but two. And then the door would open quietly and there was Gran in the doorway, not cross, just bemused. 'I hope you are playing hymn tunes, Margaret,' she would say, and return to her nap. 'Yes, Gran,' I would reply and go softly into 'Abide with me' or 'What a friend we have in Jesus'. Very daring, I would jazz them up, just a little bit – they always sounded so much more interesting with a definite beat accompaniment! But the soft pedal, or rather the soft stop, would be out – I never pushed my luck. So many things were just 'not done' in my day, and being wilfully disobedient was one of them – especially to your Grandmother!

But on the other days at Grandmother's, I was allowed out into Gran's garden, unfettered and unrestrained. My favourite pastime was to play 'concerts'. My stage was a strip of tarmac and my only prop, a small chair. Gran and Great-Aunt Fan were again having a snooze, so I was never interrupted or observed. I liked to pretend to be Fred Astaire, performing my party piece: 'I'm putting on my top hat, fastening up my gloves' – I knew all the actions as I had seen the film through at least twice – one could if one had the stamina and inclination! But my tap dancing was very poor in heavy shoes (my mother did not approve of my *learning* to tap dance). I expect you are wondering why I had taken out the chair; this was for the audience – me – where I would sit, in turn, and be very generous in my appreciation, transported into the realms of make-believe. I would have been about eight or nine at this time. I never had an audience!

In old age, wearing a long floral dress and usually an overall, perhaps with a chenille short jacket, with her hair piled on her head and with a narrow band of velvet at her throat, Grandma spent the rest of her days visited by her family, one of whom called in every day.

> A verdict of 'death by misadventure' was recorded by Bournemouth co-roner (Mr T. C. Thompson) at the inquest on Mrs Mary Ann Carter (91) who died on Wednesday after a fall at her home on November 4th. She fell and fractured her right arm.
>
> Dr G. S. Scott said death was due to heart failure accelerated by the shock of the fall.

So ran the report of the accident in the local evening paper in 1953.

The tragedy happened this way:

On the fatal day, when Great-Aunt Fanny was out shopping, it was decided by my Grandmother that the baking of jam tarts was the order of the day. Now the jam, home made of course, was housed in a high cupboard, making it very difficult for Gran to reach it. Nothing daunted, Gran got out her 'steps'. This comprised a large wooden chair with arms, on which was placed a child's chair. Gran had done this manoeuvre many times, always successfully. But this time, the chair wobbled and she was thrown to the ground. Here she had to remain until Aunt Fanny returned.

My mother told me that as she bent down to hear Gran's final words, she noticed a look of supreme contentment come over Gran's face as she uttered one word over and over again: 'Up, up, up.' We like to think she had met her Maker.

I knew that Grannie cared deeply for us all, although she never showed it outwardly. We rarely kissed, and never embraced. Her love for us all showed in a thousand kind ways.

Schoolmistress, Church Organist and Dance Instructor

Bessie Marguerite Davis (1872–1949)

Bessie was at the centre of every activity in her village.

y paternal Grandma could not have been more unlike my mother's mother, in almost every way. For example, my father's mother was a staunch member of the Church of England (in fact, she was the Church organist) and my mother's mother was a member of the exclusive Plymouth Brethren.

Dad's mother, Bessie Marguerite Davis, was born in 1872 in Ryde, on the Isle of Wight. Her father was formerly butler to Sir George Cornewall at Moccas Court, Herefordshire. At one time he was valet to Lord Portman.

I did not know my Grandma for some years! She strongly disapproved of my mother marrying my father. 'Don't you realise,' my mother was told, 'that you are taking my only son away from me?' The die was cast after that remark!

Both my parents kept a discreet distance from Gran after they married, but the family did meet up again twenty years later, at the outset of the Second World War, when I was ten years old. A chance meeting made the reunion possible.

Gran lived in Bournemouth and was born into a household with high aspirations. Her sister Agnes went to teachers' training college. Her first post was the school at How Caple, Herefordshire. Later, Gran joined her.

It was here that Gran met and married my Grandfather, where they set up home in Yatton, the next village. This tiny hamlet must have been kept alive by my Grandparents' activities. Not only was my Grandfather the wheelwright and gamekeeper to the Big House but he was also sexton for the Parish Church and taught dancing in the village hall. He charged sixpence a lesson. Grandma meanwhile ran the village school from the schoolhouse. She had been asked to take on this task by the lady from the

Bessie Marguerite Davis with her school, 1898.

Big House, Lady Clive. The school photograph shows twenty very healthy looking children in their best clothes, and my Grandma. Years ago I traced the house and adjoining school and was invited inside. I noticed that the marks which the pegs for the children's coats had made were still visible. The pupils came from the surrounding farms and had to bring their own dinner with them. Grandmother never spoke about her teaching days to me.

After early Communion in the parish church, at which Gran played the organ, she would invite the curate to breakfast. He was a bachelor. Among the breakfast fare would be St Ivel's best butter which, my father said, was never present except on Sundays! The curate would retire to the garden privy after breakfast, smoking strong tobacco.

Sadly, my Grandma died in her early seventies, red-haired and very strong willed almost to the end. She lived alone after Grandad died in 1925. We never knew the details of her mystery foster child who was about four when we met up again with her in the forties. At the end of her life she lived with her daughter. I remember Gran's lovely complexion and sweet smelling powdered face, with her red hair piled high on her head.

My mother often told me a story that when she had not been married very long, Grandma, who then lived in the next road to us, took a taxi to visit us, bearing a rich Fuller's cake! Such extravagance was beyond my parents' comprehension!

One afternoon stands out in my memory, showing Gran's generosity. Funnily enough, cake featured in this incident also.

It was nearing the end of the Second World War. Food was scarce. I was a schoolgirl. After playing games all the afternoon in the school field near where my Grandma lived, I thought I would pay her a visit, and took my best friend along with me. Not only did Gran give us each a very strong cup of tea, which was very welcome, but she also cut the fruit cake she had just baked – in half, and gave it to us to eat! Of course, we cut it in half and had half each. But the memory of that wholesale largesse remains with me. A quarter of a cake each . . . unbelievable!

As Gran entered her late sixties, she went to live with her daughter as has already been mentioned. Sometimes Gran would come to tea with our family and I would walk her to the bus stop and make sure she got on the right bus.

How I would love to have heard stories of her past life, her days of teaching, playing the church organ, instructing the dancers. But she never said a word.

She died peacefully, in Christchurch Hospital, aged seventy-seven.

Bessie Marguerite Davis

The Owner of the Beaded Bag

Fanny Saunders (*c.* 1850–1910)

Leaving France in order to marry a gentleman's valet, Fanny encouraged her daughters into the teaching profession.

y Grandmother, Fanny, was French, from a well-to-do family. She came over to the Isle of Wight as a young girl to visit the Portman family who were staying in Ryde, on holiday from Bryanston, their country seat near Blandford, Dorset. There Fanny met Lord Portman's valet, Rodney Saunders, and fell in love. He had also been valet to Sir George Cornewell. They married on the Island, where three children were born: Agnes (my mother), Bessie Marguerite, and a baby boy who died.

Fanny had three brothers – one who designed the first yacht to sail the Atlantic and another who wrote poetry (to my sorrow my copy of one of his books got lost in the final break-up of my home). The third brother was a gentleman of leisure. They never visited us, or we them.

My Grandmother spoke perfect English, without a trace of accent. Moving from the Island, my Grandparents settled in Bournemouth, Dorset. My mother, Agnes, married in 1900, and my Grandmother who, as I have said, came from a wealthy family, gave my parents a house as a wedding present. After some years, my parents moved to Alma Road, still in Bournemouth, to be nearer to my Grandparents. As young ladies living on the Isle of Wight, my mother and her sister were known locally as 'the two young ladies of Ryde'. They must have cut splendid figures, one blonde and the other a fiery red-head.

Back to Fanny. She was very graceful, had a rosy complexion, and was always very dignified. Her pancakes were superb! She was always very generous towards me, giving me 2*s.* 6*d.* per week pocket money. My mother gave up telling me to save it – it all went on sweets and cakes! Grandmother's dress was of black silk, and on her belt she hung a jet-beaded bag, hand-sewn, with a fringe around it, also of jet beads. In this bag Grandma kept her handkerchief, nothing else. I treasure it still. Grandmother also taught

Fanny Saunders. She married Rodney Saunders who was valet to Lord Portman at the time. He had been butler to Sir George Cornewell, of Moccas Court, Herefordshire.

me to read before I was five years old. I would sit on her lap, with the simple reader before us, following the words with my finger. She was very patient with me. Grandfather also was very keen that I should be aware of things, especially nature. I remember on one occasion, when I was very small, Grandad and I were in their garden, and a passion flower plant was growing up the brick wall at the top of the garden. Grandfather picked one and explained to me why it was called a passion flower, with the reference to Christ. He was a very gentle man.

In their old age, my Grandparents came to live with us. They gave my mother's sister, Bessie Marguerite, their house, as they had already given my mother a house on her marriage. Grandmother died of a stroke as she was sitting in the kitchen. On the day of her funeral, when I was about seven or eight, Mother gave me a note to take to the haberdasher's, for a pair of white stockings in which to bury my Grandmother. Grandfather died sometime afterwards. I was grown up then, and was asked by my mother to sit with him during his last night. I remember reading and correcting school books at his bedside through the long night. I had followed my mother into the teaching profession.

Urbanization and a growing geographical mobility made it easier than in the past for sons and, to a lesser extent, daughters, to be economically independent of their parents.

Both my mother Agnes and her sister Bessie were examples of this trend. They were included in the lessons with the Portman children and their governess when they resided on the Isle of Wight, Grandfather being valet to Lord Portman, as has been mentioned. Later Agnes and Bessie were sent to a 'Dame School' on the Island – there was quite a choice in the later part of the nineteenth century. Agnes always kept her instruction books, even when she married. The expansion of education meant a corresponding increase in the number of teachers. Men and many women also were recruited (as they received less pay). When my sister and I were little, before we went to school at five, my mother would give us lessons on the dining room table, complete with exercise book and pencils. She would even ring her old school bell to summon us for lessons! We both read well before we went to school.

Before my mother married, she was a teacher at several schools in Herefordshire, Somerset and Bournemouth. But it was at Howe Caple, in Herefordshire, that she was the happiest. She shared the teaching in this

1. COWES. 2. RYDE. 3. THE ESPLANADE, VENTNOR.
(From Photographs by Messrs. Poulton & Son, Ltd.)

The Isle of Wight where Fanny and Rodney Saunders first met

village school with her sister Bessie Marguerite. Bessie was not a trained teacher, but had been asked to start a school in Yatton, close by. The family pun – the play on words, which we said *ad infinitum* – was 'How caple [capable] are you!!' We though this very clever! The sisters had a happy time here at Howe Caple, going into Hereford on foot every Saturday afternoon, shopping, and walking back again. It was here in Herefordshire that Bessie met her husband, George Claud Charles Hodges Davis, who was a cabinet maker at the time.

My mother married Joe Barrett much later on, who was lodging at the time with my Grandparents. He (my father) suffered with his chest and needed the 'high' air of Winton. He later developed a thriving photography business there. In the First World War he had instigated some of the first X-ray films in France, where he was staying in a château with other soldiers. A titled lady had taken some of her friends and was running a hospital there. Dad sent examples of the X-ray films home to us, in a box with a false bottom! Unfortunately, I have destroyed them, not thinking that they would be of any value now.

But back to Fanny Saunders.

I think of my Grandmother with deep affection. It never occurred to us to wonder why we never met her French family. Perhaps they 'cut her off', as the saying goes, for marrying an Englishman without many prospects.

Yatton, Herefordshire. Village life in 1898–1914

Bessie Marguerite Saunders had moved to How Caple, Herefordshire. While here, Bessie met George Davis in nearby Yatton. Life in that village portrayed a pattern of life now gone forever.

George Claud Charles Hodges Davis and his father were employed on the estate of Sir George and Lady Clive, of Perrystone Court. The Clive estate encompassed property in three villages: Yatton, How Caple, Upton Bishop and a part of Foye. The majority of people on the estate were employed by Sir Clive as tenant farmers. Sir Clive's staff were as follows: Miss Gizler, a German lady, was employed as a companion to Lady Clive. German governesses and companions ceased to be the fashion only with the First World War; not until the Germans began to be our enemies overnight in August 1914 did the Victorian admiration for them cease. The

From the Hampshire directory 1857. Acknowledgement and thanks go to Hampshire Record Office, Winchester, for permission to reproduce same

Queen was never so happy as when she accompanied the Prince Consort to Hanover to which her ancestors belonged.

The most senior of the servants would have probably been the butler. House staff comprised two ladies' maids, two parlour maids (receiving £12 per year plus their keep), a cook, a scullery maid and two footmen.

A coachman and his assistant looked after the horses. The Clives' first car, the first private car in Herefordshire, was purchased just before 1914.

The garden was extensive. Among the gardening staff, the head gardener reigned supreme. In the greenhouses were grown choice flowers and grapes and the orchid house kept four men in full employment. Six men looked after the kitchen garden. The head gamekeeper at this time was George Davis Senior, who had three assistants.

At the apex of this large estate and responsible for the smooth running of it was Mr Herbert, whose efficiency enabled the Squire to go shooting, in season, or go abroad for two months in the summer.

George Davis, Senior, died in 1922 and his gravestone is the first nearest the church door in Yatton churchyard.

Bessie Marguerite Davis (whose mother was French) ran the village school at Yatton; her son was brought up in the school house. Bessie was granted ten tons of coal yearly to keep the school and house heated. She might have been employed by the State, the Church or by Mrs Clive. Bessie taught the three Rs and singing (she always kept her tuning fork), until the school closed in 1911 through lack of pupils.

Bessie was head of the Mothers' Union and played the church organ. She helped her husband with his dancing class. The commencement of the First World War was just around the corner.

Bessie, her son and her husband returned to Bournemouth to live.

The French Connection

Helena Lindsay (*c.*1877–1949)

Grandma was religious, but she never went to church. She had her reasons.

My Grandmother, Helena Lindsay, was born *c.*1877 and died in 1949. Her mother was French, and I well remember as a small child being taken to see my Great-Grandmother who lived in a small cottage in Fishbourne, near Chichester. She talked about the hard times she had had during the siege of Paris when they had to eat dogs and cats. My Grandmother married a merchant seaman and had seven children between 1897 and 1908, my mother being the eldest.

My Grandfather died before the First World War; Gran spent the War on munitions at Vospers. During this time, she met Jim Lindsay, a Master-at-Arms in the Royal Navy. Gran took his name, but it was not until after she died that anyone knew that they were not married. When Grandfather retired from the Navy, he and Gran took a job as joint stewards at a Working Men's Club in Slindon. After this they moved to Millcot and my Grandfather worked on the estate of Lord Moyne.

My abiding memory of my Grandmother is of a small round lady, always dressed in black, standing at the sink and pumping the water. There were very few facilities, only gas. The toilet was the privy down the garden. Every day Gran cooked the food for her large number of chickens. I can still smell the concoction!

Gran was religious, always humming hymns, but I do not think she ever went to church, though she made sure that the grandchildren went in the care of our maiden aunt.

All twelve of us grandchildren spent part of our summer holidays at Millcot with our Grandparents. We had complete freedom and spent a lot of time collecting wood from the spinneys for the copper and fires. Looking back, this must have been the highlight of our young lives.

Gran was the matriarchal figure who never went out. Once only, when a son-in-law took her to Bournemouth on a short trip, did she venture outside her environment. Two daughters were married from Millcot, but Gran did not attend the church services, staying at home to prepare the wedding breakfast. The fact that she was not legally married must have haunted her throughout her life.

Gran never went shopping. Everything was delivered – meat, groceries, bread. All other purchases were made by the carrier who shopped for all his customers in Chichester. The items he bought included clothing and household requirements. When Gran needed his services she put a card in the window for him to call.

Finances were obviously tight. Gran sold eggs and fruit from her orchard, at the door. My Grandparents were self-sufficient in vegetables from their very large garden.

When the Train played Cupid

Martha Frith (*c.*1880–1940)

Martha's relationship with Grandad had a stormy beginning but a happy ending.

 ur Gran lived with her unmarried sister, who was rather delicate and possibly bullied 'for her own good' by Gran (Aunty Ruth was a little airy-fairy).

Gran was a tenant of a house in Stewart Road, Bournemouth. She was a very good cook; in fact she had been one before she married. The kitchen range cooked lovely meals; rice puddings especially always tasted wonderful cooked this way. Every weekend she would buy a piece of brisket from the local butcher who would not have dared to sell her a tough piece of beef. During the following week we would hear her say to her neighbours, 'I bought a piece of brisket about this big' – and would measure using her forefinger, the length from her fingers to her elbow. This brisket would be slowly cooked in the range and the fat saved for a fruit cake, which never rose very high but always tasted very good.

The kitchen range was lit late on in the morning and banked down in the afternoon, when the rice puddings were cooked. It was heated by coal, and one day a week when Gran and Aunty Ruth would go to the cemetery to tidy the family graves, the range would be heated with fir cones, which they collected from the cemetery grounds. Nothing was ever wasted.

My Gran loved a bit of gossip, but would never admit to eavesdropping, so it was always, 'When I was shaking out a duster, I heard . . . '

Now and then my Mum and Dad, who was an engine driver, went on holiday on their own, whilst I went to stay with Gran and Aunty Ruth. Though their routine would be entirely different with me staying there, they always made me feel very welcome, even taking me with them weekly to the cemetery. I remember being very puzzled about the wording RIP, until Gran told me that it meant 'Rest in Peace'. When Mum and I visited

Gran, mostly on a Wednesday, Gran would always tell us where to sit, and there we sat.

Both sisters died together in December 1940.

My Grandfather and Grandmother's story is a little unusual, to say the least.

Let me explain.

My Grandfather, Walter Frith, was born in the 1880s in Bournemouth, Dorset. He was a fireman on the railways. My Grandmother, Martha Fulljames, worked in the kitchens in the numerous hotels there. But on Sundays, whenever possible, Martha and her friend would worship at the East Cliffe Congregational Church in Holdenhurst Road, Bournemouth. Now one Sunday morning, my Grandfather, always a practical joker, wanted to attract Martha's attention and, sitting in the pew behind her, stuck a long hatpin into her bustle. Although he and his friends thought this very funny, Martha did not, and at the end of the service, she swept out of the church without a backward glance at him, refusing to speak to Walter ever again.

Things moved on for my Grandfather, and in time he gained promotion to engine driver, moving to Southampton. He met and married a girl from the Winchester area. They had three boys, my father being the youngest.

By chance, Grandfather Walter was moved down to Bournemouth again, to Stewart Road where, to make ends meet, Gran took in a lodger: in fact, Walter's fireman. Then something disgraceful happened. Grandfather's wife and the lodger ran off together! Well, my Grandfather tried to keep the home going, with the help of kind neighbours. One evening when he and his friend, another fireman, had shunted their train into the old West Station, and had some time to spare before their next journey, the friend turned to Grandfather and said, 'My girlfriend lives close by. Why don't you come too. There's a kind-hearted cook there, she'll give you a hot meal.' So they went.

And as Grandfather entered the kitchen, who should be standing there but, yes, you've guessed it, Martha Fulljames, the girl whose bustle he had stuck with the hatpin. As they say in all good novels, 'they fell on each other's necks.' Having listened to Grandfather's sorry home life, and having wasted so much of her life, Martha took action. She drew out all her savings and got Walter a divorce. She kept the newspaper cutting reporting it till the day she died.

Back she went with Walter after they were married, and managed him and the three boys, who accepted her well, with a firm but kindly hand. There was never any need to take in lodgers!

Dentures and Hearing Aids

Eliza Elizabeth Blandford (1880–1963)

Eliza played her part in village life – but what part was it?

y Grandmother was one of eighteen children. Not all of them survived. Gran was born in Dorchester and in due course, leaving school, she was employed as a housekeeper to a titled family. On leaving this post to set up home with my Grandfather, she was allowed to take with her the contents of her room – the curtains, the carpet and the furniture. She also brought home a delightful ormolu clock, which is heavily gilded and highly ornamental. I have it still.

Granny and Grandad set up home in a small cottage in Dorchester, Dorset, where they had one son, my father. But the marriage soon faltered and Grandad, who was a heavy drinker, left home, never to return, although I think he still kept in touch. My Grandmother then went to work as a housekeeper at Athelhampton, Dorset, the medieval manor house close to the main Dorchester/Bournemouth road. My father, by this time, was despatched to boarding school, where he stayed until old enough to join the Royal Navy. He rose through the ranks to become a commissioned officer, having married my mother in the nineteen twenties. He was posted soon afterwards to the China Seas, where his ship saw service for two and a half years. It was here that he contracted TB which finally killed him.

My mother nursed Father over a long period at home, and in order to get some respite from looking after us and my father, my brother and I were sent down from Portsmouth to stay with 'Grandmother Blandford'. Gran had by this time left Athelhampton and was living in Dorchester. She let her large shed-cum-barn to owners of pedigree dogs, when their pets were in season!

I remember Gran used to keep on her dressing table a silver brush, comb and mirror set, on the back of which were the initials E.E. I asked her one day, what the initials meant and she said 'Eliza Elizabeth'. The very next birthday card I sent to Grandma I addressed her as 'E.E.' Gran was *not* amused; in fact she was very annoyed!

Gran was a bookworm. Her favourite author was Sir Arthur Conan Doyle (especially his Sherlock Holmes stories) and she enjoyed reading the *Strand* magazine in which his stories were printed. In her cottage there was a bookcase on the stairs leading to the bedrooms where, among other books, was a large edition of *The Snow Queen*, with a white and gold leather cover. I would sit for hours on the stairs reading this book.

Gran's brother-in-law, Fred, lived next door and kept chickens. Many a time Uncle Fred and I would seek refuge in the chicken run, away from Gran! I would be hiding from her because I had incurred her displeasure for some reason, and Uncle Fred because he wanted to light his pipe – Gran forbade smoking in her house. We would have a quiet chuckle at our daring!

The room in which Gran lived had a cupboard which ran the length of one wall. In it she kept pillow cases, sheets, spare linen and lots of false teeth and several hearing aids. When Gran died, and my mother had to clear out the cupboard, she found that all the linen had disintegrated with age, and the various sets of teeth and hearing aids had to be hastily discarded into the dustbin. The contents of that cupboard always fascinated me. The false teeth, the hearing aids, the sets of highly starched linen – where did they all come from? Was Gran a 'laying out' nurse? Was she often called out to perform duties? We were never aware of this, but we always had to be in bed at a certain time, and much earlier than was our custom in Portsmouth.

Gran was very strict with us, and made sure that our manners were impeccable. Although she was not religious, Gran insisted that we said Grace at every meal – 'For what we are about to receive . . . ' My mother always said that she doesn't know how she would have coped if Gran had not had my brother and me to stay for long stretches at a time, when Dad was so ill. I think I get my love of reading from Gran. I see her now, her head constantly in a book. It was her only way of escaping from reality.

The 'Angel' of the Hearth

Gwendoline Jones (c.1850–1940)

When the children asked 'Is your Gran in?' and the answer was 'yes' they would flee.

My Gran was born in the middle of the nineteenth century; she was ninety when she died.

Granny married a Sergeant-Major in the regular Army, by whom she had ten children. On his retirement, Grandad bought a public house, the Ormsgill Arms, in Barrow-in-Furness. Later, my parents took over the pub, and I remember my Grandmother (who was eighty at the time) sitting in her rocking chair in the scullery adjoining the public bar, divided from it only by a flimsy curtain. As she gently rocked, she would knit furiously, like Madame Defarge. She was never without these huge knitting needles which looked like drumsticks (and were used by us as such when we got the chance) and thick dark wool. To complete this picture of industry, Gran smoked a clay pipe – in fact she was never without it.

What with the gloom of the room, painted in dark colours, the smoke, the dark knitting, and the pipe, it was quite a Dickensian scene. To cap it all she kept a brass stair rod to hand, and if any of us fourteen children incurred her wrath, she would lash out – and she never missed! And if, by some chance, she was unable to deliver the stroke, she would bide her time and seek redress on another occasion. Children who came to play would say, in a very quiet voice, 'Is your Gran in?' – if the answer was 'yes' they would flee. Even the regular customers in the bar would comment, 'Ma's smoking that pipe again!' as the evil-smelling smoke escaped from the depths of the scullery with Gran puffing away like an engine as she knitted.

But it wasn't always 'Hard Times' at the Ormsgill Arms. Although Gran was outwardly stern, she often gave us small sticks of cinnamon which she would fetch from the bar, and a halfpenny or a farthing would be handed over with great love and affection.

Grandad's Army training never left him. He was a formidable man; he never smoked or drank and ruled the roost when he was alive.

But Gran and her clay pipe remain in my mind to this day; smoking, knitting and ready with the stair rod.

The State Registered Nurse

Mary Augusta Surridge (1855–1943)

Her parents had to keep her.

y maternal Grandmother was born in 1855 in Hornsey, North London. Her parents kept a bakery where Mary Augusta, on leaving school at the age of fourteen, helped in the business.

But not for long. She decided that she would like to become a nurse. This was not a popular decision with the family, for they would have to support her. Nurses were very poorly paid; in fact, nursing began by rich women who nursed out of the kindness of their hearts. However, my Grandmother was resolute and started training at Queen Charlotte's Hospital in London, becoming a State Registered Midwife.

Not long afterwards Grandma married Fred Surridge, a master carpenter, and had three daughters, my mother being the eldest. They were not very old when their father died. So, what did Grandma do? She returned to Queen Charlotte's Hospital and packed the girls off to boarding school. Grandmother never spoke of these days except to say, 'You don't know what hardship is' to my mother, and later to me. After boarding school, the girls entered domestic service.

But the strong streak of determination was alive and pulsating in my mother, as will be revealed in the following account.

At one of the many visits my mother made to a London theatre, she met my father, who was a Royal Groom at the Mews in Buckingham Palace, and married him. In order for the pair to live in the Royal Mews, my mother had to be interviewed by a Palace equerry. If she 'passed muster', when there was a vacant dwelling in the Mews they could set up home there. She was accepted. Two boys and a girl were born, I was the girl, and we all attended the church school at Eaton Square.

And now this is where the streak of determination raised its head. Mother went out to work. This was unheard of. An equerry got to hear of this and told her to stop working, but my mother refused. He explained that it

Mary Augusta Surridge

wasn't allowed. Eventually the news reached Queen Mary, Father's employer, who asked to see Mother. Queen Mary said, 'Why are you so poor? Don't we pay you enough?' And my mother explained that she wanted her children to be educated. The consequence was that Queen Mary set up a scholarship in order for the Royal Household children to benefit.

I met Royalty often, when they came to the Royal Mews; one of the first things I had learnt to do was to curtsey. The Princes and Princess were often visitors to the Mews, viewing the horses, and when we were addressed we would reply with a 'Ma'am' or 'Sir'.

Queen Mary always looked stern, but she was very interested in her staff. Every year, then as now, a garden party was held to which we were invited, always remembering to keep in our allotted place, which was cordoned off. The Royal Party sat on a stage, receiving foreign dignitaries only, but on one occasion, they received a little blonde girl of two and a half – me! I had slipped through the cordon, escaped from my brothers who were in charge of me, run to the stage where Queen Mary and King George V and their party were seated, and practised my curtsey in front of them. Queen Mary saw me and said to an equerry, 'There's a dear little thing, bring her here – and get her an ice-cream.' This was done. When my family discovered where I was, they were most apologetic, but Queen Mary explained, 'We invited her up – eat your ice-cream.'

Later we discovered that Queen Mary had sent for the Royal Photographer, Winnie Broom, to take our photographs. 'Then I shall know them and I shall ask after them,' said Queen Mary.

Strong willed women run in our family. I am very proud of the way my Grandmother and my mother stood up for what they considered, against opposition, they thought was right, my Grandmother to become a nurse, and my mother to go out to work although wives of members of the Royal Household were not allowed to.

Grandmother died aged eighty-nine years, in 1943.

The Dressmaking Genius

Elizabeth Powell (1878–1968)

She never used a paper pattern – yet her garments were a perfect fit in every case.

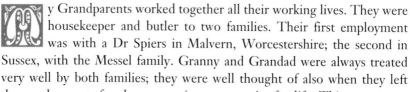y Grandparents worked together all their working lives. They were housekeeper and butler to two families. Their first employment was with a Dr Spiers in Malvern, Worcestershire; the second in Sussex, with the Messel family. Granny and Grandad were always treated very well by both families; they were well thought of also when they left the employment, for they were given an annuity for life. This was not an uncommon occurence.

The Messel family, in particular, treated my Grandparents well, so much so that, when my mother was old enough to receive schooling, she was invited to take lessons with the children of the family and their governess. Mum was very happy here, but when the children left to go to boarding school, Mum was sent to the local school, where she was terribly teased about her accent and general demeanour. However, it stood her in good stead when she left at fourteen and sought employment at a local fashion house. She accompanied the buyer to London each month, to select clothes for women who were going on cruises; they would buy a complete wardrobe for each client. Cruising was a popular pastime for the leisured rich in the twenties. Later on, Mum learnt to drive a car – Dad taught her. It was unusual for a 'working girl' to be able to drive, before the Second World War. Dad was keen on cars.

When Grandad died, Gran came to live with us. We lived in Bournemouth then. Mum had a hard time keeping harmony in the home and Dad always managed to keep out of Gran's way; this wasn't a hard thing to do in the war years, as he was in the Air Force. During this time, Mum got a job with the civil service and Gran looked after us whilst she did so. She was insistent on my having a good education, as she saw the value of it. She encouraged my mother to send me to a fee-paying grammar school.

Not long after my commencement at school, the Education Act of 1944 decreed that the fees should be abolished, but uniform, of course, had to be purchased.

Grandmother could cut out and sew any garment to fit the wearer. The unusual facet in this dressmaking story was the way in which she would cut out each garment. She never used a paper pattern. Her method was to place the material against the back of the sofa and, without the aid of pins or marks, she would unhesitatingly employ the scissors with utter confidence. I always marvelled at her ability. The garment was a perfect fit in all cases.

My mother, too, inherited an eye for fashion, but she did not possess Gran's skill with the scissors.

Grandma and Grandad were always very particular how they were dressed. Walking along the cliffs on a Sunday afternoon, they made a fine pair! How they conducted themselves in public was also important to them. Neither attended chapel or church, but they never stopped my mother and me going to the local Anglican church.

Gran died in 1968, having lived with us and weathered the changes of addresses we had when Dad was a publican, for nearly twenty years.

The Small Dynamo

Mary Ann Cross (1846–1925)

Grandma was a 'monthly' nurse

y Grandmother was born in Whitchurch Canonicorum in 1846, the only daughter of a farmer. She had the unusual disability of being born with her left arm finishing below the elbow. This did not prevent her from doing anything a normal person could do with two arms. She could knit and sew, holding the knitting needle in the crook of

Mary Ann Cross pictured with her youngest grandchild. Notice Gran's left arm is concealed by the child.

her left arm; when she was sewing, she would put on a leather shield over the stump, and rest the material on that. She also had a treadle sewing machine. Settling in Southampton, my Grandparents had twelve children, seven of whom lived beyond infancy.

Gran was a 'monthly' nurse, which was different from a midwife; when a woman had a baby, Gran would visit her for a month, keeping her eye on mother and baby.

Unfortunately, Grandfather, who was a railway guard, died whilst the family were still young. Gran was awarded an annuity from the railways of 9s. 2d. per week, but her hardships did not prevent all her children receiving a good

The family of Mary Ann Cross in mourning for their father

standard of education in Southampton. All the girls were apprenticed to tailors, one boy became a headmaster and another had his own business.

When my Grandfather died, all the family went into mourning for a year. The girls wore plain black dresses for six months, after which time a pretty coloured collar was added, or perhaps a brooch.

Every Sunday, after morning service (Gran was Church of England) and Sunday School in the afternoon for the children, the family, *en masse*, would troop up to the cemetery on Southampton Common where Grandad was buried. This routine never varied.

Granny was very strict. As grandchildren, we knew not to stand on her left side, for her stump was far more painful than her right arm, when she lashed out at us!

Gran's eldest son was six feet tall – Gran was not quite five foot three. On one occasion, we were all assembled for her birthday, and my uncle said something to which Gran took great exception. She turned to him and said, 'You may be as big as a house, but when you're in my home you won't say things like that – or I'll come and thump you.'

Her sayings were, 'Little girls should be seen and not heard,' 'Mind your P's and Q's,' and 'Sit up straight.'

Granny's pastry was superb. She made mince pies for the whole family at Christmas. I used to stone the raisins for the mixture, but I was never allowed to pop even one raisin into my mouth. Her eagle eyes were everywhere.

The whole family spent Christmas afternoon with Gran. The 'girls' of the family would make the tea and the 'boys' would wash up afterwards. The evening was spent playing rhyming games and singing around the piano.

Grandma would get me to fetch this mixture for her cough from the chemist's. She supplied the bottle to put it in. The recipe was as follows: 2 pennyworth of oil of violets; 2 pennyworth of syrup of squills; 2 pennyworth of camphorated oil; 2 pennyworth of oil of almonds; 2 pennyworth of ipecacuanha. The chemist would hand me the bottle, with all the ingredients in layers. It was fun to shake the bottle and watch the mixture blend.

My Grandmother always wore a cape, so that her disability was never apparent. She never went out of mourning for her husband. She died in 1925.

*The coloured collar was worn on a black dress after six months of mourning.
The spectacles belong to Mary Ann Cross*

When my mother died in 1921, of peritonitis, my father wanted to marry
my mother's sister, who had never married, but the vicar refused to marry
them in his church as this relationship was not allowed, so Father went to
a non-conformist church, who had no such qualms about the legality of
the marriage.

When Father heard that he could not marry in his own church, he made
quite a spectacle of the refusal, one Sunday morning. We were all sitting
in the pews, ready for the service to commence, when Father came storming
into the church and publicly said, 'You think I am not good enough to be
married in this church, then I don't consider this church is good enough
for my family here,' and he ordered us all out of the church, never to
return.

I was mortified!

I expect many tongues wagged over Sunday lunch that day!

Mother of Fifteen

Louisa Jane Howlett (1860–1936)

Great-Grandmother said 'Louisa, you must teach the girls to keep house. They may all marry poor men!

ouisa Jane Howlett, my Grandmother, was born in 1860. Her family were farmers, living in St Germans, Cornwall. There were two daughters and one son, my mother being the eldest girl.

Grandmother met Grandfather (William) in Cornwall, but Grandfather came from Norfolk. How was this possible? Grandad owned a fleet of fishing trawlers and would arrive before the trawlers at their destination, as the boats followed the fish in due season. Louisa and William were married in the parish church of St Germans and, like Mr and Mrs Beeton (of cookery book fame), spent all or part of their honeymoon in Ireland.

On their return they set up home in Hackney, London, later moving to Walthamstow, Essex (then a village). My mother, Kate Marion, was the youngest of fifteen children, five boys and five girls surviving, and five of the babies dying stillborn, save one who was named Percy who lived for five months.

Over this large family hovered the guiding spirit of my Great-Grandmother, who lived at Saltash with her son, daughter and daughter-in-law. Great-Grandma made sure that the children were being brought up as responsible citizens and, to that end, several children of the family would take it in turns to visit their Grandma at Saltash, leaving by train from either St Pancras or Waterloo Station. They would board a 'Family Drawing Room' carriage. Food for the journey could be booked ahead and put on board at designated stops on the way to Saltash. Great-Grandmother often said to Louisa Jane, 'Louisa, you must teach the girls to keep house, they may all marry poor men!'

Back at Walthamstow, Grandmother always had help in the house. She also had the dependable Cracknell family. Mrs Cracknell and one of her daughters would appear early each Monday morning to do the washing in the copper. On Tuesdays they would return to do the ironing. As one Cracknell daughter left to get married, another daughter would take her place.

Many years later, when my Grandmother was in her eighties, one Christmas Day she presided, as usual, at the family gathering at dinner. The weather was terrible – thick fog – and she told the family (looking like the cat who had stolen the cream) that on Christmas Eve she had learnt that Mr and Mrs Cracknell were not too well (the link with the families was never lost). She had gone to see them and found them both in bed, so she had spent the evening reading the local paper and reminiscing with them very happily. Then she had returned home, on foot, which was quite a distance.

The 'Barnardo Dance' was the first public engagement attended by the five Howlett daughters as they came to suitable age.

Louisa Jane Howlett

It was held in Walthamstow. The Girls' Village Homes were down the road at Barkingside. Long after all the Howlett children were married they continued to attend the Barnardo Dance.

One story my mother enjoyed telling me was of the haywains passing the house where the family stayed as children, just outside North Weald, Essex. She well remembered the carts passing in the early hours of the morning on their way to the hay market in the Mile End Road.

My Grandmother died in 1936. She was due to move to sheltered accommodation but the thought of the upheaval was too much for her, and she died.

Everything was Wrong

Mrs Wright (*c.*1860–1930)

Nothing was ever right for Grandma.

y Grandmother was born in Grantham, Lincolnshire. She was strict, cold and ungiving. As a child, I hated her. She never attended church or chapel, and consequently did not encourage her children to attend either. My Grandparents had four boys, two of whom entered the Army as boy soldiers. Another, my father, went into the Navy and rose through the ranks to become a petty officer. The youngest lad stayed at home and became a hairdresser.

Grandad worked on the railways, and one fateful day the train in which he was travelling ran into some buffers, resulting in Grandad losing a leg. The surgeon who attended him did not do a very good job of the amputation and cut through a nerve in his leg. The result was that Grandad was in pain for the rest of his life. In those days, there was little help from the railways in the shape of compensation, thus the whole family suffered financially.

When my father came out of the Navy, we left Weymouth, Dorset, where we had had quarters, for there was no work for him. We found rented accommodation in Wimborne, Dorset. Mother was very keen that we attended church as a threesome, although Dad had never been a churchgoer. He balked at going to the Anglican church, saying that there was too much bowing and scraping there, though this was where Mum and I usually attended. So, as a threesome, we sought out the local Baptist church, and went there. Sometimes when my aunt, who had a 'paid up' pew in Wimborne Minster, could not go to church for any reason, we went in her place.

One gloomy day after Grandad died, Grandmother came to live with us. She was such a forceful woman that my mother had a hard time keeping the peace. Now, for some unknown reason, Grandmother was most particular about me keeping my toys out of sight. Certainly they were not to be brought downstairs to make the place look untidy. So this was my plan of action. I would get up early, long before Gran was about, and play with my dolls, keeping my mother company. As soon as I heard Grandma's footsteps, I would gather up my playthings, rush into my bedroom and continue the game there. Perhaps Grandmother thought that I was wasting my time playing, when I should have been sewing, knitting or making myself useful about the house. Who knows what was in her mind?

As I have remarked, Gran had no religion, and was intolerant of those who had. One example of her irritability towards anyone who showed their faith will be borne out in the following story.

One day, when I was about seven, just before the commencement of the First World War, the chance of going on a picnic came my way. This was a great treat for me. Now my mother had a little wicker basket, which would just hold my sandwiches, and I asked her if I could use the basket for my picnic. She demurred at first, but then relented when she saw my pleading face. She insisted that I take great care of it – and not lose the peg with which the lid was fastened. I agreed to all demands, confidently and quickly, in case she changed her mind. During the picnic, yes, you've guessed it, I lost the little peg! It was somewhere in the huge field in which we were playing. Although all our attempts at finding the peg seemed hopeless, I prayed fervently that it would be found. Incredible though it must seem, I opened my eyes and, just in front of me, was that little piece of wood! I couldn't believe it!

On my return home, my mother complimented me on the care I had taken of her treasure. Well, I had to own up, and recounted the story of the lost peg and the 'arrow' prayer. Now my Grandmother, who was passing at the time, heard my confession, and scoffed, 'Such foolishness to teach a child such things!' Now my mother, who always held her tongue for the sake of harmony in the home, told her bluntly and forcibly not to interfere.

Grandmother sought no love from us, not even from my father, her son, and in return, did not receive any. I think she was envious of the loving relationship which the three of us shared.

Grandmother was a sad, embittered woman, who had had to cope with a handicapped husband whilst striving to bring up four sons. It must have been one constant struggle, and because she could not be friendly with anyone, owing to her offhand disposition, it made her life the harder.

How sad that I have no memory whatsoever of any kindness shown to us. Nothing was ever right for Grandmother – save her name!

Bargains for All the Family

Lilian Emily West (1882–?)

'When Grandma papered the parlour . . . '

ilian Emily West, my Grandmother, was born in December 1882 in Dover. She was the middle child of eleven children, who were mostly girls. She married Edwin Jacob West in 1902, and they had three children: Edward, Lilian and Olive, and they also brought up Bob, the illegitimate son of her sister Rose.

Grandfather was a Master Mariner, and they moved around quite a lot during their married life. My mother was Lilian, and I was born in my Grandparents' house in Portsmouth, where they had settled when Grandfather worked on the tugs in Portsmouth Dockyard. Gran's family always lived in rented accommodation, and when Grandfather retired they took a public house on the corner of Arundel Street in Portsmouth, called the 'New House'.

By this time my own family were living in Gosport, Hampshire, and every Saturday we took the bus and the ferry and walked up to North End to visit my Gran in Portsmouth. We stayed to tea and usually had winkles and cockles, caught at Bosham by my Uncle Bob. These were boiled in a large brick copper in the back kitchen by my Gran, who taught me how to get the winkles out of their shell with a hat pin. She always buttered the bread far more lavishly than my mother, and her teas were wonderful. Often my two cousins were there, and we would all sit by the range whilst Gran told us stories of when she was a little girl. She would also recite many poems which she had learnt as a child. She was a very practical lady who did all the decorating in the house and would go to the sales and jumble sales, and find bargains for all the family. My favourite family story is of my Grandmother decorating the landing of an Edwardian house, helped by her sister Gladys, Now, my Grandfather, when he was not at work in the pub, would sit and read downstairs. This was one such time. Grandmother was decorating the ceiling, standing on a chair, which was

– 49 –

balanced on a table, almost overhanging the stairwell, aided by Aunt Gladys. Naturally this manoeuvre involved much climbing up and down to move their positions. On one occasion, as they were moving the table the chair crashed to the ground, taking Granny with it. A faint disembodied voice came up the stairs. 'You all right Lil?' My Grandmother's comments are not recorded.

I feel honoured that my mother always used to say to me. 'You're just like your Grandmother.'

A Friend to All

Constance Smith (1874–1963)

Her life revolved around her growing family. Her father was a Portsmouth City Councillor and a Justice of the Peace.

y paternal Grandmother I can remember not at all, but by contrast my maternal Grandmother was a dominant figure for the first thirty-five years of my life.

She was born Constance Uniacke, in Gosport, in December 1874, the second of ten children, eight of them girls. Her parents kept a public house, the King's Arms, in Gosport High Street. None of the Uniacke sisters went out to work, although each had to take a turn in the bar and with the housework.

Gran and her sisters used to tell of cleaning the step of the King's Arms early one morning and seeing Edward the Seventh, when Prince of Wales, walking by. I was inclined to take this with a pinch of salt until recently I heard of a house in Gosport where lived one of Edward's ladies, so maybe they did see him strolling back to Osborn House when they were cleaning the step.

Gran's father was a Portsmouth City Councillor and JP, and he and Gran's mother were known for their kindness to the poor of the neighbourhood. He often paid the fines he levied, and she kept a table at the side of the pub where the poor could always find food and clothing. This compassion was no doubt passed on to my Grandmother, because she was extremely soft-hearted and, although far less comfortably off than her parents had been, shared what she had. When visiting Gran we sometimes had to go into the parlour because Gran had asked a gypsy and baby into the living room for soup or cocoa and a warm, no doubt saying, 'Come in, my cocker!' A baby which arrived soon after marriage was known as 'a short cut across a field' and anything which didn't work was known not to 'ackle'. I can remember being reprimanded at primary school by a handicraft teacher when I said just that. I thought everyone said it!

Grandma: some of her ways

Despite the completely domestic life she led, Gran had very definite ideas and took an interest in national events. She was also a great champion of the underdog; one felt she would take on anyone. Not long ago I met an elderly man who told me how, as a child, he used to take refuge with Gran when his very strict father was searching for him with a stick.

In March 1895 they moved to Victoria Road in Springbourne, Bournemouth, Dorset, where they spent the rest of their lives, Grandfather dying in 1951 and Gran in 1963. They had nine children, three of whom died in infancy. My mother was the second eldest and only daughter, and when Gran gave birth to her last child at the age of forty-two she left the care of the infant, and most other things, to my mother. Gran was already white haired and seemed to become an old lady from then on.

She was an Anglican, but wasn't above visiting the nearby Presbyterian Mission Hall on social occasions, which goodness knows were few and far between. Apart from church and the weekly Mothers' Meeting with its occasional outing, Gran's life revolved around her family, with rare trips back to Gosport for a family wedding.

Life was very hard because my Grandfather not only drank more than he could afford to, but he received an industrial injury before retirement age, after which he never worked again and for which he received no compensation. The burden of their upkeep fell on my parents. My Grandmother seemed to take this completely for granted and as their right. Fiercely proud of her five sons, she seemed to treat my Mum as an unpaid servant before, and even after, my mother married. To me, however, Gran was most loving and protective, and I knew where to run when I was in trouble, often coming home with a crust of newly baked bread and butter from the old-fashioned baker's on the corner of Victoria Road which Gran had funded.

I always went to see Gran and Grandpa after morning Sunday School and never remember this as being a duty. Gran was a large lady with surprisingly slim legs but vast bosom. She never knew the luxury of a bathroom but kept herself scrupulously clean to the end of her long life. She always wore black woollen stockings, whatever the weather, flannel petticoats and what she called 'me stays'. A very good cook, her speciality was faggots. Gran was an expert at skinning a rabbit, cooking hearts and sheep's heads, and making quantities of Christmas puddings; I usually got the silver threepenny bit she had hidden in the pudding. It was taken for granted we went to Gran's for Christmas.

Springbourne in Gran's day had shops of all kinds. Even so, she had her definite favourites, the International Stores being one, and Ridouts the butcher's near to Central Station, although there were butchers nearer. On Friday afternoons she and my mother would often walk to Boscombe, quite a fair walk, to patronise Sainsbury's, going via Boscombe Grove Road so that I could see the sheep which grazed in the field there. Woe betide any shopkeeper, however friendly, who sold her short measure or something less than fresh!

When I read of the Abdication of Edward the Eighth, I always think of my Grandmother. Like the rest of the country, my family discussed the situation at great length, as if it were happening to one of our own. My Gran had the last word one day when talking about Mrs Simpson. 'If anyone thinks I'm going to curtsey to the likes of her,' she said, 'they've got another think coming!'

With the advent of television Gran would be found sitting in her accustomed seat by the fire, at right angles to the set and squinting at it with one eye – she was not going to change her seat. If a lady of nobility and of a certain age was featured, Gran would say, in a very authoritative tone, 'That's who the Prince of Wales should have married!' And we dared not contradict.

At the beginning of the Second World War the whole family went to the Pavilion at Bournemouth to support a charity dance. Mum bought Gran a new dress – a dark print with a white collar. One of my uncles, in his naval uniform, took Gran around the dance floor for an old-fashioned waltz. All the people clapped the old lady with the white hair and the modern dress, dancing with her son.

Three of her sons and her grandson served in the Second World War, and one day Gran made a list of all her family, including the many nieces, nephews and in-laws, who were serving in the Forces or the Home Guard. In telling folk how many names were on the list, Gran implied that without them the country would be in a very sorry state!

One of her sons was awarded the MBE in the Coronation Honours List, for work in the Consular service. First thing that morning Gran was resplendent in her best hat and coat ready to go to St Paul's School nearby, to tell the headmaster that her Billy had got the MBE. Apparently uncle's headmaster had once predicted that Billy would not progress further than entertaining at the end of the pier! It took a lot of coaxing on my mother's part to persuade Gran that if the headmaster was still alive he would have retired by now. So reluctantly, Gran had to content herself by telling everyone she met about Billy, including the bit about entertaining at the end of the pier.

Towards the end of her life Gran became very deaf, and much against her will wore one of the first hearing aids, strapped around her large waist and clipped to the front of her dress. She would not wear it outside the house and many were the embarrassing moments as she became more deaf and her voice louder. She was never one to mince words, so often folk she met would say, 'You must come and have a cup of tea with me,' without a definite date. Next time she met them and when they were scarcely out of earshot, she would boom, 'That was a blooming fine cup of tea we had, wasn't it?'

Gran was a lovely lady and much mourned when she died. We shuffled a bit in our pews though at the funeral service when the vicar referred to her straight talking. What had she said to him, we wondered.

Gran has been gone more than thirty years now, but when the family meet we still talk about her. The memories are of happy days.

Kinswoman
of Charles Haddon Spurgeon

Agnes Wright (*c.*1840–1923)

My Grandparents brought me up – and spoilt me!

or the first years of my life I was brought up by my Grandmother, who in 1862 had married Clement Wright, the cousin of Charles Haddon Spurgeon, the great Baptist preacher.

Although at the time of their marriage, Grandfather owned a butcher's shop at Horndon in Essex, he then bought a pub called The Swan (where my mother and two aunts were born) and also the farm opposite the pub; a cowman lived in the farmhouse and managed the farm. I remember that we used to go by wagonette to Colchester to visit relatives.

How did I come to live with my Grandparents? Owing to my father's serious illness, Grandmother took me to live with her when I was one year old. After my father's death, a year later, my mother returned to The Swan to live with us.

Before she married, my mother worked at Parnell's, a large fashionable store in Victoria, London, where all the society ladies would shop. One day I went there with my Grandmother, who embarrassed me exceedingly by lifting up her skirt in order to reach her under-petticoat, where she kept her purse, in order to settle the bill. She never carried a handbag.

Although my Grandfather was Baptist and my Grandmother Church of England, they both attended Gran's church on the rare occasions when they *did* go to church. Curiously, in an age when rivalry between different schools of Christian belief was intense, Grandfather was very keen for me to attend the Established Church.

Gran had help in the house: a woman came to do the washing on Mondays in the huge copper in the scullery, returning on Tuesday to do the ironing.

Grandmother was a tall lady, very upright, standing five feet ten or eleven and much taller than my Grandfather. She was always telling me to 'pull my shoulders back'. Grandmother was well educated, as was her sister, who went on to own two grocery shops in Woolwich.

I shall never forget the death of my Grandmother. I found her, fatal victim of a massive stroke, sitting in her chair near the fire. I was devastated – I lost my father so early; now Gran had gone! I was eight years old.

When I was eleven, my mother married again. There were seven more children of this union, but two were stillborn. I visited the family occasionally, and got on well with my step brothers and sisters. I had been thoroughly spoiled by my Grandparents, which caused great displeasure to my stepfather as I could not abide by his rules. For example, in his household it was butter for the grown-ups and margarine for the children. Of course I was used to butter back at The Swan and told him so. I was also given plum jam, which I loathed, and asked for strawberry. As I had started a new private school when my mother re-married, it was decided that I had better stay at The Swan, which was nearer the school. Hurrah!

My Grandparents were very good to me during my childhood. Of course I missed Grandmother terribly when she died, although she was stern, like many Victorians, but she and Grandfather gave me a comfortable home and the warmth of their love.

Gran's Gran had Nursed with Florence Nightingale.

Patience Julia Priscilla Wilson (1862–1954)

Patience was married at sixteen to a widower with a son of ten.

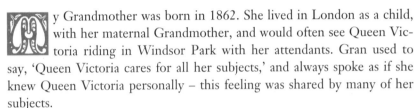y Grandmother was born in 1862. She lived in London as a child, with her maternal Grandmother, and would often see Queen Victoria riding in Windsor Park with her attendants. Gran used to say, 'Queen Victoria cares for all her subjects,' and always spoke as if she knew Queen Victoria personally – this feeling was shared by many of her subjects.

Gran expected to work hard for little return, and did not envy those with a better way of life. Gran's Grandmother had been a nurse in Salisbury and, although she was not a nurse in the Crimea, had worked with Florence Nightingale during a smallpox epidemic in the town. Florence Nightingale at one time was staying at Wilton House nearby.

This Grandmother, Grandmother Holly, had a daughter who was pregnant and due to be married. Her husband-to-be was overheard boasting in the local pub that he would 'bring her to heel' once they were married, whereupon Grandma Holly refused to allow her daughter to marry him. No member of her family was to be 'brought to heel'. The daughter, who never married, became a nurse in France during the First World War. Gran Holly was related through marriage to Professor Fawcett, whose statue stands in Salisbury market square.

Gran Holly, through nursing, introduced my Grandmother to a widower who later became her husband. Gran was sixteen years of age. Samuel Wilson was an engine driver who had a ten-year-old son. The family went to live in Templecombe in Somerset, in a railway house close to the edge of the platform. My Gran had five children and fostered two, a boy and a girl. The girl, when ten years old, went to join her mother in Canada, and

Patience Wilson (on the right)

the boy subsequently joined his father, after the Great War. Gran employed a woman to do the washing for sixpence a week plus her dinner.

In time, with her family grown up, Gran came to live with us. In fact, she took care of us, as both my parents worked, as did my aunt, in business. Gran ran the house, did all the cooking and shopping, and generally ruled us with Victorian firmness.

We always went to Sunday School and Church, but Gran didn't come. However, she had a firm belief in 'The Almighty' and in a life hereafter.

Gran prepared the breakfast for all the family around 7.30, and made sure that everyone got off to work or school on time. At 11 o'clock sharp she had a half pint of Guinness and some bread and cheese. Gran retired to bed in the afternoon, having cooked the dinner, to read her romantic novels. She then set the tea. At nine o'clock she had another bottle of Guinness and bread and cheese, and with a candle to light her way, retired to bed.

She used to say, 'Laziness is not worth a tinker's cuss unless it is well carried out.'

When Gran went shopping, she wore a calf-length black silk coat and felt hat, and always carried a small purse. Indoors, her long-sleeved dresses were protected by a wrap-over cotton pinafore. She changed her dress in the afternoons without fail.

She died in 1954.

The Delicate Wife

Kate Parkin (*c.*1870–1930)

Gran held the family together whilst Grandad left to build the railroads in Canada.

 his is my Grandmother's story, gleaned from overheard conversations and chance remarks.

I was six years old when my Grandmother died, and had it not been for her poor health, our family might have been Canadian.

Grandma was born in Barnstaple, North Devon. She was a children's nurse with a nursery maid to help her. She was never very strong, but she was held in such high esteem by her employers (the family were 'in timber') that they built a lift, leading to the nursery, so that Gran did not have to climb flights of stairs.

Grandad and Grandmother married in Barnstaple, where they met, but sought better prospects in Bristol; here Grandad went into partnership. Unfortunately this did not work out; the story went that he was cheated. However, with six children to bring up – three boys and three girls, my mother being the youngest – Grandad decided to emigrate to Canada. He wanted the whole family to go with him, but the doctor advised my Grandmother against taking such an uncertain step. So Grandad went alone to Winnipeg, where he stayed for five years, building the railroads. This meant that he could save, having only himself to keep, and send money home.

Back in Bristol, Grandmother kept the family home going. She was very fond of music and saw to it that each child was taught some form of instrument. My mother played the violin and had ballet lessons. The family visited the Colston Hall, Bristol, and once saw Pavlova dance there.

The children were given their allotted tasks to do each day. One of my mother's jobs was to clean the knives each week in the knife machine. The stained and blunt edged knives would be inserted separately into the circular machine. The handle was then turned, and when the knife was pulled out

The Parkin family in the Great War

it would be cleaned and polished and sharpened. No stainless steel in those days!

When Grandfather returned home from Canada, he was met by all the family at Avonmouth Docks, in Bristol. It was hard to recognise the healthy-looking man who stepped off the ship, in his lumber jacket and with his fresh complexion. He looked so Canadian!

Every week, Gran went to Old Market Street, in central Bristol, for her meat and butter. Other days she shopped locally. Sometimes the relations who still lived in Devon sent cream from the country. A treat indeed!

Not only did Gran suffer from her digestion, for which she claimed bananas gave her instant relief, she also had a goitre in her neck. To hide this, she wore high-necked collars.

Grandma had some wonderful sayings. 'No one is going to stop their horse a-gallop to look at you,' and 'You'd stay there until seven stars come to fourteen!' This was when my mother was not getting a 'move on' – call it a bedtime dalliance. And another saying: 'If you haven't changed your underclothes and have an accident, I shan't own you.' This was a constant worry to people who might have to attend a relative after an accident, to find the victim wanting in the clean underwear department!

Sundays were held in great respect in the Parkin family. No sewing or card games were allowed. But strangely, it was only Grandma who attended the Methodist Chapel on Sunday mornings. The children were not forced to go with her.

Wash day on Monday, ironing on Tuesday, Gran did it all on her own. When Grandad returned from Canada, he brought with him a washing-machine – a wooden tub with a handle, with paddles which pushed the clothes to and fro. It was quite unique in the neighbourhood. On Tuesdays, when Mum came home from school, Gran was still ironing till gone four o'clock.

Sadly, poor health and hard work took their toll. Grandmother died aged only sixty.

My Welsh Inheritance

Catherine Hardiman (1883–1982)

Gran lived with us all my life. Her influence on us all was considerable.

y Grandmother Catherine Hardiman, née Roberts, was born in Mountain Ash, South Wales, in 1883 where she attended the local school until she was twelve years old.

She then went into the millinery business, making ladies' hats; she also attended sewing classes, sang in the choir and enjoyed dancing. She was a staunch Baptist all her life, regularly attending the services at the local Baptist Church. Granny enjoyed her work as a milliner, so much so that many years later, when Grandad's family were on their way to start a new life in New Zealand, they sent back some lovely ostrich feathers from South Africa, to trim the hats Gran made.

At nineteen Granny met and married my Grandfather, who worked underground as a pit manager in a coal mine. They had five children. The first-born were twins, a boy and a girl. My Grandparents were too poor to raise both of them, and so Granny's mother-in-law, who lived a few houses away, took in the little girl. Sadly she died, at the age of twelve months, from pneumonia, and as if by telepathy the little boy living at home pined away and died soon after. My Grandmother went on to have three more children, and, as was often the case in those days, several miscarriages.

Life was hard in those times and Granny took in washing to make ends meet. But on one gala occasion, when visiting Tonypandy, my Grandparents saw Queen Mary and King George V when they opened the new Town Hall.

During the twenties, in the Depression, Granny's daughter, my mother, who was now married, decided to come to Bournemouth to live, my father having found work as a waiter in one of Bournemouth's large hotels. He worked there, save for the war years when he was in the Navy, for the rest of his working life.

Catherine Hardiman with the twins which she lost in infancy

Grandma: some of her ways

My parents liked Bournemouth so much that they sent for my Grandparents. They all shared a house and this arrangement lasted until both my Grandparents died, Granny aged ninety-nine.

Both my Grandmother and my mother attended the Baptist Church in Winton. In fact, my Grandmother was a founder member in 1930, when the church was but a small tin building, before the brick church was constructed. Granny was also President and Vice-President of the Women's Fellowship for many years.

So I grew up in this extended family atmosphere – although I was an only child I was never lonely. I was spoiled and cosseted, as only children often are.

Granny was always immaculate and her standard of hygiene was high. All the hot water came from kettles boiled on the gas stove, as was most local families' routine at the time. Granny had a sewing machine, a treadle, which she kept in the window of the back room that was my Grandparents' domain; we lived in the front of the house. She made all my clothes.

My Gran had several fur tippets – they were stoles made from the entire skin of the fox, including the head. The stuffed head was used as a clasp, the other end hiding a clasp in the tail. Those fur stoles were draped round the shoulders and were very fashionable, being worn summer and winter. When Granny was young, she wore a pince-nez. She used Phul-Nana face powder, which came in the form of a little book, with the leaves impregnated with the powder. Her favourite colour

Catherine Hardiman as a young girl

was purple, and she loved to wear long, dropper-type earrings, of which she had many pairs. She always shopped at the Co-op and cooked lovely Welsh cakes, apple tarts, blackberry-on-the-marm and delicious cawls, a stew made of lamb bones.

Grandma had a sharp tongue at times, and would say with some vehemence, 'Speak as you find.' 'Locking the stable door after the horse has bolted' was another favourite quotation. Her influence on my life was considerable.

A Typical Welsh Housewife

Emily Lemon (1878–1961)

Gran organised everyone; she was so proud of her household management.

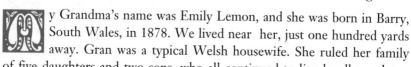y Grandma's name was Emily Lemon, and she was born in Barry, South Wales, in 1878. We lived near her, just one hundred yards away. Gran was a typical Welsh housewife. She ruled her family of five daughters and two sons, who all continued to live locally, and was the undisputed head of the family. She trained all her daughters in house-keeping and cooking.

She dressed in dark colours, and never went out without a hat. She always looked neat. She had sound common sense, which I admired. She went to the Baptist chapel on Sundays, and did the washing on Mondays. She went everywhere on the bus. Whist was her favourite game.

We loved to listen to her stories about when she was in service as a young girl. She was so proud of her household management.

My memories of her are fond ones. I was taught to fold the sheets properly after ironing them, under her eagle eye. She doted on the youngest member of the family, a boy, and he could do no wrong. It was a family joke.

All family occasions took place at Gran's house, and she continued to organise everyone until she died of a stroke in 1961, at the age of eighty-three.

A Child Factory Worker

Mary Elizabeth Harrison (*c.*1860–?)

Life was always hard for Grandma. At ten years old she was a nursery maid. At twelve she was working half-days at a factory.

y maternal Grandmother was Mary Elizabeth Harrison. She first married a Mr Healey and lived in Oldham, where she had four daughters: the eldest was my mother Dorothy, then came Ethel, Freda and Alice.

I do not remember my first Grandfather, as he was in the regular Army; he always said that he joined up to get away from the all-female household! He died whilst in the Army.

Grandma's second marriage to Joe Harrison soon followed. He was a roadmender and it was my job to take his dinner to him, whenever he was working nearby. Granny wouldn't let him go without a hot midday meal. The dinner was put in a white basin covered with a red spotted cloth, and Grandma would tell me where I had to take it. Grandfather was always looking out for me.

Grandma was a very dominant woman and made all the decisions in the house. Every day she would donkey-stone the front step, the window sills and the pavement just in front of the house. Heaven help anyone who tried to walk on the clean pavement.

To clean the steps, the white sandstone block would be rubbed all over the area needing cleaning, after it had been soaked with water; we were all proud of the brightness.

Another chore was on washing day, when we worked the washing with a 'posser'. I loved doing this. Let me explain. A posser was a copper cone on a stick which would swish the washing in the tub to get it clean. But before this operation, the washing had to be scrubbed, separated and laid out on the kitchen table. We scrubbed the washing using hard soap and an equally hard scrubbing brush – every crevice had to be explored inside and out. You must remember that there was no Clean Air Act in those days and the soot from the factory chimneys was indescribable. It was a hard task to keep things clean.

My Grandmother didn't attend church, but she favoured the Methodists.

She always wore a crossover overall and on Sundays would also sport a row of jet black beads, which I treasure to this day. She was meticulously clean, and often I stood and watched her standing over the washbasin with the water running down her arms and dripping off the end of her elbows.

She often told me stories of her earlier life. She started work at ten years of age as a nursery maid looking after children. At twelve, she was working in a local factory, half days. The other half of the day she attended school. At the age of twelve many children would work half-time: half a day in school, and half working in the mill. The system finally ended in 1921. At thirteen years of age the children became 'full-timers'. Some of the children were so tired that they often lay down among the cotton waste on the factory floor, in a corner, and fell asleep. The overseers were very hard men; they often abused the children who were too frightened to report them.

In fact, my Grandmother's sister, Auntie Fanny, had been abused at the age of fifteen by her uncle. As a result a baby was born. A good friend of the family, a middle aged man recently bereaved, offered to marry Fanny and bring up the child as his own. This he did. In middle age, Fanny went blind and to her dying day believed that it was God's punishment to her for all that had gone before. The curse of Eve accepting the guilt. My mother told me this story when I was grown up.

Another story she told to me was about my other Grandma and her husband, who was killed at Passchendaele in the First World War. When his 'effects' were sent home, my mother said that there was nothing there that had really belonged to him. The horror of that ghastly war made it an impossible task to return the effects to their rightful owners. To show the feelings of those times: my Grandma was married again at thirty-four (after all she had three children to bring up) to a churchgoing widower, but her family never spoke to her again. They thought she should have remained a widow in memory of her fallen husband.

But to return to my Grandmother born Mary Smith. She had a beautiful singing voice and I often got her to sing just for me. I think she identified herself with Gracie Fields whom she knew. She was passionately fond of opera, and knew many of the classic arias. She also loved the theatre and

Mary Elizabeth Harrison

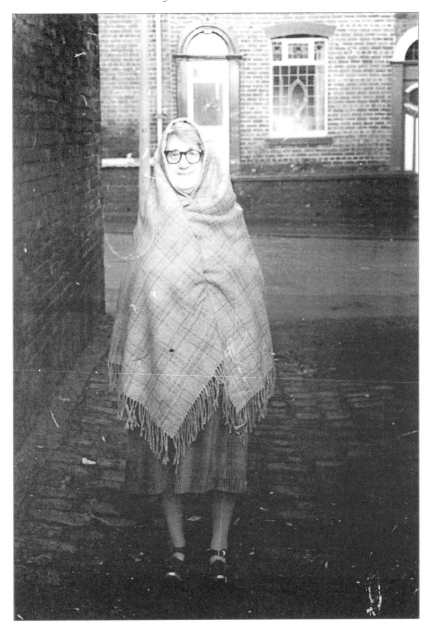

A north country woman in traditional shawl and clogs

the cinema, nursing a secret love for Errol Flynn. But my, was she sharp tongued. I can vouch for it!

But life was hard for Gran. It was a job to make ends meet with a family to feed. One day Gran, overburdened as ever, threw down a sixpence at my mother's feet (who was about eight at the time) and said, 'See what you can do with this.' My mother went to the butcher's where she bought two pennyworth of bones, then on to the greengrocer's where she purchased a pennyworth of potatoes and a pennyworth of vegetables. She was so proud to bring home twopence change!

The Depression came in the twenties, and the family were forced to go to bed early to save the gas lighting. My father was made redundant the day I was born and did not get another job until I was five years old. During the time he was out of work, my mother got various jobs, one being as a spearmint chewing-gum salesman going from door to door. There was always the means test lurking behind every job Mum got. Sometimes they were a shilling worse off, as the government allowance would be docked. So many men used to drink that the wives dreaded pay day, when the men would collect their wages from the 'office' – they would then come home and beat up the wives and children in their frustration because they had no work. My father was not among such men.

But then my parents heard of a wonderful town being built called Luton, with a factory making Vauxhall motor cars. We came down south and for three years Dad was in work there. Then we moved again to Frensham, Father having found an even better job.

Hard Times

Elizabeth Passills (1863–1945)

At thirteen, she was a dancer in the chorus of a local theatre. She met her future husband there, known as 'Stage Door Johnny'.

y Gran was Elizabeth Passills, always known as Liz. She was born in Portsmouth in August 1863. At nine she was working in a drapery store in Portsmouth. At thirteen she was a dancer in the chorus of a local theatre. Here she met her future husband when he came round to the stage door. Thereafter, she called him her 'Stage Door Johnny'.

Grandma had five children, and when Grandad died she took in washing to help out; she was also often called on to sit with people who were dying, and afterwards she would prepare them for the undertakers.

Although Gran was baptised into the Baptist Church, she was not a regular church attender.

When she grew older and more frail, Gran came to live with us. She always looked smart, and never ventured out unless she had powdered her face – with fine chalk! Living with us Gran did not have to cook or make any decisions, but she did like to wander round the shops, which were open before the war until ten o'clock at night. She also enjoyed a good weepy at the cinema, or a funny film. Gran's infectious laugh made everyone else laugh who heard her!

Gran liked a little drink at lunch time. We would get her a half pint of porter from the Bottle and Jug, where in the evenings she would meet her friends and have a good gossip. When Gran was eighty, she had to have her leg off, so we then took her about in a wheelchair. This did not deter her going to the pub most evenings when, on the journey home, she would sing all the way!

Gran enjoyed plays on the wireless, and especially Radio Luxembourg. Most Sundays I would read to her – she enjoyed a good love story, and would comment on all the character as I read.

Gran died in 1945, leaving twenty-eight grandchildren and twenty-six great-grandchildren. She was a lovely lady, very fair minded, lots of fun, and we loved her very much.

Days Spent in Blackmoor Vale

Elizabeth Warr (*c.*1860–?)

The memory of the contrast between that golden vale where I spent my holidays, and the seemingly vast 'sea of houses' where I lived, remains with me.

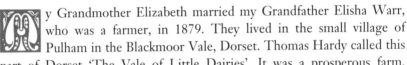y Grandmother Elizabeth married my Grandfather Elisha Warr, who was a farmer, in 1879. They lived in the small village of Pulham in the Blackmoor Vale, Dorset. Thomas Hardy called this part of Dorset 'The Vale of Little Dairies'. It was a prosperous farm, enabling the three sons to attend Sherborne College. My mother went to school in Dorchester. My Grandmother died soon after her last child was born and my Grandfather married the housekeeper at the next farm. They had two children. I always looked on my Step-Grandmother as my 'real' Gran.

My Grandfather, a churchwarden, was a respected member of the community. On Sundays he always wore a black coat and a red or yellow spotted waistcoat when he went to church. Grannie was dressed in black. She had her own dressmaker who made her clothes, and ours, when we lived there.

My mother married a farm labourer from her father's farm, who had left school at eleven years of age. His father had been let down over a business deal, so my father had to leave school and take the only job available in that small village – farm labouring. At the beginning of their marriage, my parents lived in a house provided by my Grandparents, but when the eldest child was born, my parents decided to uproot themselves and seek pastures new in Boscombe, Bournemouth which, at the turn of the century, was expanding. It was still not easy to find employment and Father was forced to make a living by cleaning carpets. He would collect the carpets from private houses and hotels on a hand truck and wheel them down to the cliffs (we lived nearby). He would proceed to beat the carpets by hand – there were few vacuum cleaners then. Sometimes he had to collect at five o'clock in the morning – no wonder we were all in bed, including my parents, by 9.30 each evening! Soon he branched out as a chimney sweep and because he was so clean in his work and never left soot on the carpet, he was much in demand.

When I was three years old, my mother, who had contracted consumption, was ailing. Having had nine children, she was now unable to do very much work around the house, and so it was decided that my sister (a year older than me) and I would stay with my Grandparents in Pulham until it was time for us to go to school, then we would have to return to Boscombe.

You can imagine that after being one of nine children in a comparatively small house, to be sent to a working farm in the country, with me the centre of attention, seemed like paradise. I was spoilt, petted and generally fussed over. Haymaking and picnics, making the cheese and butter in the dairy – all the seasons had their own beauty and charm. When I went to market with Grandma we went in the carriage which was upholstered and padded, drawn by one horse called Joe-Joe – he was mottled.

I remember that house so well. The scullery with the flagstone floor had a little pump at the butler sink. Grandmother had a woman from the village to do the rough work and another woman came to help with the milking. There were about thirty cows, as well as poultry and sheep.

There were two four-poster beds in the farmhouse, with blue curtains which I loved to pull around me – one bed was made of mahogany, with furniture to match, and in another room there was the oak four-poster with matching oak furniture. In each room there was a wash stand with two washbasins in each with matching ewers and chamber pots.

Granny made me wear gloves to church and I had to keep the dresses and bonnets clean which the dressmaker had made for me – no hand me downs here!

It was a far cry from the house which I had left. I wasn't homesick. Indeed I didn't want to return to Boscombe – I cried, I grizzled, I fought, but of course I had to do what I was told, and back I had to come, to go to school. I never really recovered from the two extremes of living, the sunlit Vale of Blackmoor and the 'sea' of houses at Boscombe. Over and over again I repeated homeward-bound on the train, 'Bricks! Bricks! Bricks!' I was allowed to return to Blackmoor Vale in the long August holidays – how I longed for the time to come round, and how quickly the summer days flew by. To reach the farm, we were put in the charge of the guard at Bournemouth Central and my Grandparents would meet us at

Sturminster Newton Station, the nearest to Pulham. Oh, the freedom of the countryside, the kindness and love of my Grandparents, no household chores – there was always help there – no worries – just complete serenity.

And then in 1920, when I was fourteen, my mother died, aged forty-four. As Father married soon after, my sisters and I decided that our stepmother wouldn't want us, so we left to go into service. I was maid to a doctor's family who treated me very well. But even now, in my eighty-ninth year, I think about those golden days with my Grandparents in the Blackmoor Vale. It was truly another world.

Perhaps Elizabeth Warr's granddaughter captured the same feelings here at Pulham, in the lovely Blackmoor Vale, as did Thomas Hardy's heroine Tess, in this special kind of agricultural landscape:

Either the change in the quality of the air from heavy to light, or the sense of being amid scenes where there were no eyes upon her, sent up her spirits wonderfully. Her hopes mingled with the sunshine in an ideal photophores which surrounded her as she bounded along the soft south wind. She heard a pleasant voice in every breeze, and in every bird's note seemed to lurk a joy.

Tess of the D'Urbervilles: 'The Rally'.

Two Strangers in a Strange Town

Emily Sarah Botto (1873–1956)

Grandma married a member of an Italian Army Band.

y Grandmother, Emily Sarah Heap, married Francesco Botto, who came from Italy to play in the Bournemouth Municipal Band under its first Musical Director, Dan Godfrey. Bournemouth's first public music was provided by the Italian Band, which came for a winter season in 1876 and stayed for sixteen years. The musicians, who wore uniforms of the Italian Army in which all had served, entertained on the paddle-steamers and gave subscription concerts. They often played from a gallery over the Gervis Road end of the Arcade. In 1892 the town established the country's first Corporation band of twenty-one players, under Signor Bertini.

The next year Bournemouth Corporation took over the Winter Gardens. Here the Bournemouth Municipal Band, including my Grandfather, continued to delight the growing audiences.

How did my Grandmother meet Signor Botto who was living in Bournemouth? Grandma was born in Reading in 1873, of Catholic parents, and came to Bournemouth to work when she was sixteen. Of her family she said very little, but on occasions she remembered her poor but happy childhood in Reading, and told me of her journeys to the factory of Huntley and Palmer, the biscuit makers, in order to buy broken biscuits for the family.

Having attended one of the Corporation concerts, Grandmother met Signor Botto, fell in love and married. They were both Catholic and also both were in a strange new town. At the time, my Grandmother was seventeen years of age. Three sons and two daughters were born to them, my mother being the youngest child. Grandfather enjoyed cooking, especially making spaghetti bolognese – he taught my mother to make the dish, who always cooked it 'just like papa'. Although, unhappily, Grandfather left my Grandmother whilst the children were still at home, and she was

The Botto family, 1903

forced to take in paying guests, Grandad kept in touch with the family, and did not completely abandon them.

Grandma never lost her sense of humour, and was always smartly dressed, great fun to be with, and interested in music, the theatre and whist.

Of course the family were brought up in the Catholic faith and when my mother wanted to marry my father, a Congregationalist, she was excommunicated. This meant that she was more or less excluded from taking Communion at her church. The effects of excommunication affected the person's right to receive the sacraments, or Christian burial, until the individual repented or was reconciled with the church. This was always a great sadness to my mother. She sometimes took me to the Sacred Heart on Richmond Hill in Bournemouth, saying, 'We'll just slip in at the back.' She was always very anxious that she should not be recognised, but found great comfort in her actions and the church surroundings. However, just before she died, Mother received the last rites according to the Catholic Church.

It must have been so hard for my Grandma, at seventeen, alone in a new town, taking on marriage with a foreigner, a temperamental musician. Through it all, though, she never lost her spirit and sense of fun.

She died in 1956.

Co-driver of the Bean

Hannah Mary Stark (1872–1944)

Grandmother would wave to the patrolmen when saluted. She felt just like the Queen.

y Grandmother, Hannah Mary Beaumont, was born in 1872 in Yorkshire. She married twice. Her first marriage was to a Mr Hurd and when he died she was left with two young girls, my mother Violet and her sister Ada. Grandmother had to take in washing to support herself and her daughters. Later, Gran went as a housekeeper to a family named Stark, whose trawler business was based in Hull. After some years, Grandma married Mr and Mrs Stark's son Walter, who joined the Royal Navy as an engineer, prior to the First World War, then the family came to live in Portsmouth. As we lived a half hour's walk away from my Grandparents, we used to visit them about three times a week. One highlight of these visits was seeing the first wireless set there (before they were available to the public) housed in a dark walnut polished cabinet. After tea, my parents and Gran would sit in the dining room whilst my Grandfather would fiddle with the 'cat's whisker' until we heard music – oh, what a wonder it was, and what important people my Grandparents seemed to me!

They also owned an open-tourer red 'Bean' motor car, which was a two-seater with a dicky seat at the rear. What a grand spectacle my Grandparents made as they trundled down the road at the speed of 20–25 m.p.h., with Gran sitting upright on the left of my Grandfather; what a performance when he wished to turn left! Sitting in the dicky seat with the dog, I heard everything that was being said. 'Stand by, Nance,' Grandfather commanded, 'We are going to turn left, give the signal, arm in.' My Grandma took her motoring responsibilities very seriously. For these trips in the car she would always wear a musquash fur coat and a pillbox fur hat. I never remember the hood of the car going up, so they must have only taken the car out in fine weather! The car was sold in 1928.

Grandma: some of her ways

When my Grandparents took the Bean out, with me in the dicky seat, my parents had to follow in their motor bike and side car. This was a black and green Royal Enfield, the side car being an open wicker-work chair into which my mother had to be fastened with a broad brown leather strap. My father used to grumble at having to follow my Grandparents as they drove so slowly, as the exhaust fumes used to make his eyes smart!

In those days, the AA used to salute members. My Grandmother used to wave to patrolmen when they saluted, just like a Queen! As my father was a police constable in the Portsmouth City Police Force, my parents often attended Police Balls and I was sent to my Grandparents for the night. My mother would then collect me the next morning, taking me to school if it were a weekday. How I used to look forward to those visits. I would play cards with my Gran in the evening, have a lovely supper (Gran, being a Yorkshire lass, was always cooking), after which I was put to bed with a stone hot water bottle, in a soft feather mattress. I used to sink into this warm bed, Gran would kiss me goodnight and always say, 'Sleep tight, hope the fleas won't bite!'

Gran loved the Hippodrome in Portsmouth Guildhall Square. My Grandparents had a permanent booking of two front seats in the dress circle every month. If a seat was available next to them they took me.

Gran gave me my first taste of whisky. I used to do her shopping on Saturday mornings. She gave me three whole pennies – no wonder I thought she was rich!

Gran enjoyed taking snuff. Sadly, this habit lead eventually to her painful death from nasal cancer. She was under the impression that it cleared her head. The snuff came in a little metal box, which was lined with dark blue glass. Inside the box, also, was a little silver spoon with which she spooned out the snuff onto the back of her hand. She then inhaled the mixture of tobacco, first one nostril and then the other.

I inherited, among other things, my Grandmother's beef dripping pot. In those days, Gran always had a brown rounded pot full of lovely beef dripping. When my family visited my Grandparents, we came home with a pot of beef dripping. When Gran died, my mother used it. In turn, it was passed down to me. Just a plain little pot, but I still cherish it and still use it only for dripping. Each time I use it I think back to my childhood. The pot must be over one hundred years old. Not worth a lot, but a treasure for me.

An Introduction to Wine

Emily Head (c.1870–1952)

Grandma was a dominant woman: she held bridge parties. Sunday mornings we would all meet at her house.

y Grandma, Emily Head, was born in Plymouth, Devon. Five children were born to her and her first husband – Cecil, Frank, Percy, Vera and Rita. Cecil was killed in a road accident when his nanny was taking him out in his pram. Gran never got over the accident.

Grandma's first husband was a pawnbroker in Devonport. After he died, my father went into business at the age of thirteen years. He was subsequently left a sum of money by an aunt with which he changed the business into a gentlemen's outfitters.

Grandma remarried and every Tuesday she would hold a bridge party in her house, which seemed filled with knick-knacks and photographs of members of the family. Grandma was a dominant character and was always smartly dressed.

My happiest memory of Gran was when all our cousins met at her house on Sunday morning with their fathers (mothers must have

Emily Head's family

– 81 –

been preparing the Sunday roasts). Gran gave us all a 'port and lemon' which was a very unusual thing to do; we loved it. Gran's house was bombed during the Second World War, but she survived the bombs by being under the stairs.

She died in 1952.

The photograph shows me in Grandfather's arms.

The Punter

Eliza Voisey (1880–1970)

'Where's Gran?' we would ask. The reply was always the same one. 'Gone to back a horse!'

y Gran was born in Exeter, one of six sisters who were very close to each other in age and temperament.

When Eliza married my Grandfather they came to live in Bournemouth. Eleven children were born to them, nine of who died young.

While Grandfather was alive, my mother would take us to visit them regularly at their home near the Upper Pleasure Gardens on Saturday afternoons. My father 'worked nights' on the Hants and Dorset buses, so he needed his sleep during the day. The distance to Gran's was about three miles from our house, and although we took the short cut through Meyrick Park, the journey always seemed endless to me, as I clutched the side of the pushchair in which sat my sister and brother. Being the eldest certainly had its down side!

But all those journeys ended when the Second War began. Grandfather, who was never very strong, had died a few months before the hostilities started, and so Gran was invited to come to live with us, and have her own 'bed-sit'.

Every day Gran walked the short distance to the shops in the main road, frequently stopping to gossip with anyone who had the time, and so catch up with the news. She always bought a daily paper, not to see how the war was progressing (or even if we had won the war!) but to check which horses were running – she so enjoyed a flutter! Whether or not she was ever successful, we never knew, but if we ever asked where Gran was, Mum would say, 'Oh, Gran's gone to back a horse.'

Gran loved jumble sales, and often took me with her. She wore layers of clothes and sometimes topped her new outfit with a shawl. A second-hand clothing store which had recently opened above a shop near the traffic lights in Winton, Bournemouth, was where Gran most liked to go, to be kitted out at bargain prices. Although I went with her, I was never bought anything!

St Luke's Church of England claimed Gran's allegiance, but her visits here were not so regular as the others I mentioned!

We usually had a cooked breakfast; although the food rations were small, bread was plentiful, and we occasionally had an egg, a slice of bacon, or a sliver of cheese. There was always toast, even if there was not much to put on it.

And what was Gran, meanwhile, doing in the scullery whilst we were waiting for our breakfast? Getting in Mum's way, and holding up the proceedings. Gran would be curling her hair with meat skewers! She would put two or three skewers in the flame of the gas to heat them up and, when the temperature was right, she would hold them with a cloth, one at a time, and curl the front of her hair, to frame her face in frizzy curls. The back hair was ignored – being taken up in a bun. All the time this was going on, we had to sit waiting for Mum to present us with our breakfast. Mum (being her daughter) was under Gran's thumb; she never reprimanded Gran or reproved her in the name of hygiene. Even when Mum had given us *carte blanche* over something, Gran would disapprove and forbid us to do it. I really resented her. Gran wasn't too keen on my father, who sensibly kept out her way!

However, most of the day Gran kept to her bed-sit where she kept her butter ration next to Wright's coal tar soap, a habit I didn't like or approve of. I also disliked the bucket which she kept under her bed. But Gran, who had a good voice, sometimes sang to us, mostly First World War songs, and the house livened up a little then.

After the war was over, Gran went to live with her sisters in Exeter. She died in Park Prewett Hospital, Dorset, of a stroke, in the early 1970s.

But to this day, whenever I see a metal skewer, I think of Gran, and how we waited, like hungry chicks in a nest, for Mother to feed us.

A Quiet Woman

Charlotte Louisa Rosina Bedford (1888–1949)

Her Great-Grandma came from Ireland. Great-Grandfather was in the Dragoon Guards.

harlotte Louisa Rosina Bedford, my Grandmother, was born in 1888 in Funtley, near Fareham, Hampshire. Her mother had been born in Ireland, and was a midwife; she made her home in England after marrying my Great-Grandfather, who was in the Dragoon Guards. During the Second World War I often stayed with Gran, sharing her bed.

Gran attended Funtley School, Fareham. She also attended the Anglican church nearby. Every day, without fail, she took Epsom salts in the morning and Beecham's Pills at night.

She made all the decisions in the family. Gran's dresses came down to her ankles, and she was never without a pinafore – the cross-over kind which elderly people wore. She walked everywhere and shopped at the local village store, where, among other things, she purchased her one real pleasure in life: a packet of Woodbines.

Grandmother died in 1949.

An Admirer of Winston Churchill

Gertrude Bestow (1874–1965)

She was born on the same day, and within a few hours of him.

y Grandmother, Gertrude Bestow, who was one of thirteen children, was always proud to have been born on the same day as Sir Winston Churchill and within a few hours – 30 November 1874.

When Gran was eighty, we all went up to Nottingham to celebrate her birthday at a local hotel. We had her favourite meal – roast duck and green peas. Gran was thrilled to receive a congratulatory telegram from Sir Winston. Like him, she died ten years later, at the age of ninety.

Gertrude Bestow, possibly on her wedding day

During my childhood war time made travelling difficult, so most memories of her are from after the war. My Grandmother would come to Berkshire to us for a couple of weeks in the summer, or we would go up on the train to Nottingham. A great adventure! My picture of Grandma is of a slightly built, busy and bright person, always cooking or doing the washing and ironing. She lived with my aunt, uncle and cousins, and in the evenings they often played cards, especially whist. Gran defied the health and safety experts by smoking, even in bed. She also loved Guinness, and drank a glass most days.

She was terrified of thunder and would hide under the stairs. Everything metal had to be cleared when there was an imminent storm, even cutlery had to be put in drawers. My mother inherited this fear of thunder. My father had no time for such phobias, and would crash the piano keys to make us all jump!

Her Secret Lineage

Emma Knox (1880–1970)

Gran only ever spoke of her immediate family.

Emma Knox, my Grandmother, was born in 1880, and lived in Morpeth, Northumberland. She attended the Church of England. Caring for her family of six kept her very busy, but she did go shopping in Newcastle, or nearer to her home in Morpeth. Saturday was her shopping day. All decisions were made jointly between her and Grandad, who was a miner.

Grandmother only ever spoke of her immediate family. Where her family came from was never discussed, not even with her own daughters. The way she kept the house, and the quality of her table linen, coupled with her general demeanour, suggested that her social background was above that of a miner's wife. It would appear that her family disowned her when she married, but we never knew for certain.

Grandma had many sayings, one of which was, 'When you eat alone, always lay the table as if you were expecting guests.' Her neatness could not be faulted and she always set herself a high standard.

She lived to be ninety years of age.

First World War Widow

Annie Maud Coker (1883–1970)

Grandad was a PT instructor in the 1914–18 War; Gran worked in Portsmouth Dockyard during that time.

y Grandmother was born Annie Maud Ripley, one of twelve children, on 5 June 1883. The family had fallen on hard times owing to unscrupulous financial dealings. When Gran left school, she first worked for a doctor's family, and then as a waitress.

Aged twenty-two she married Charles William Coker, a Physical Training Instructor in the Royal Navy. They had two children: the eldest daughter, my mother, married Cecil Brown, LRAM; Gran's younger daughter never married.

My Grandmother, who was widowed in 1915, had a psychic experience at the exact moment of her husband's death – he died in Gibraltar.

It was a hard life in Portsmouth, bringing up her two daughters on a naval pension of which 11s. 0d. went in rent. During the First World War. Gran worked in Portsmouth Dockyard's engineering workshops, and after the War, when men returned to their families, took in summer visitors to make ends meet. Gran never remarried, was a wonderful single parent, and made the most of her life in extremely hard circumstances. Occasional holidays with relatives in Emsworth or London and outings to Portsdown Fair provided a change from the daily routine.

Gran was devoted to her family, and was particularly thrilled when her second great-grandson was born on her birthday.

Gran was a first class whist player. I used to spend hours playing cards with her, and often accompanied her to whist drives, where she seldom left without winning a prize. She had a great love of sport, particularly horse racing, and often visited Goodwood in her younger days.

As a child, Gran recalled playing with hoops, tops and diabolos, and of course, skipping and hopscotch, all toys involved having to be carefully packed away after use. Gran was a stickler for dress, and would always change out of her 'work clothes' after lunch. She never went to church, but led a Christian life, never smoking and only drinking on special occasions.

All her life Gran was frightened of thunder, and in the event of a thunderstorm would cover up all the mirrors, and then sit under the stairs until the storm had passed over. She loved crystallised ginger, steak and kidney puddings, and strong tea. When I was a child she would bring me up bread and butter with sugar on it, with my early morning cup of tea. She always put a sweet under my pillow at night, and continued to do this with my own children when she came to stay.

At teatime, when my mother was a little girl, Gran used to have a teapot and three cups and saucers on a tray. She always poured her own strong cup of tea first, then would add more water for the girls. The tea cosy was then replaced and she would prop her magazine against the teapot, place her pince-nez on her nose, and begin to read. This was her quiet period, and woe betide her daughters if they made a noise!

Grand died aged eighty-seven, in 1970.

Her Family were her World

Isabella Pashley Brocklesby (1874–1952)

Gran coloured her hair blonde until the day she died.

 y paternal Grandma was Isabella Pashley Brocklesby. She was born in 1874 in Sheffield, Yorkshire, where she lived until 1921, when she came to Bournemouth, Dorset with her husband. They then lived in a cottage in Talbot Woods.

Grandma was very up-to-date; she coloured her hair blonde until she died. She also liked to be called 'Grandma Brock', not Granny.

Her great interest was in her family. Living almost in isolation in Talbot Woods – there were only a few cottages scattered there – the highlight of her year would be the family Christmas party. I well remember them, and

Three generations: Isabella Brocklesby and my mother as a child (right); Great Grandmother with another grandchild (left)

the journey back home in the darkness, with my brother in his pushchair and me grizzling with tiredness. But Dad would keep our spirits up by telling us stories, mostly about the First World War when he was a soldier in France. He would make me shut my eyes, and he would lead me, just as his father had done for him. It made the homeward journey less tedious.

I would think of the times we stood round the organ at Grandma Brock's, with song sheets collected from the *News of the World* to help us sing the words. Afterwards, the grown ups would have supper, which consisted of cold meat and mashed potatoes.

In 1952 the milkman found Grandma Brock dead in her kitchen. She must have tripped and hit her head on the gas oven. Her poor dog was starving. We brought him home and looked after him.

It was a sad time for us all.

The Grandma whose Every Minute was Precious

Margaret Jordan (1865–1940)

Grandad had been a minister in the Lake District.

y Granny, Margaret Jordan, was born in 1865 in Manchester. My mother was christened Margaret Jordan and I followed the tradition being named Margaret Jordan also.

I do not remember my Grandfather, but although Granny died when I was twelve years old, I do have vivid memories of her.

We lived in Middlesex, and saw Gran about four times a year when we went to stay with her in Manchester. It was quite an adventure getting there. My father would take Mother and me in the car to Euston Station, and on our arrival at Manchester we took a taxi to Granny's house.

We were all Methodists. Grandfather had been a minister in the Lake District. On family occasions, at a funeral or wedding, everyone would gather round the large dining table maybe twenty people – and we would all sing the Grace. Two members of the family were in the Hallé Orchestra Choir and the Grace sounded really wonderful. It remains in my mind to this day.

Granny was asthmatic, for which she took tins of Potter's Asthma Cure, which resembled snuff. Granny would put some of the powder in the lid, then set light to it. As the powder burnt and vaporised Granny would inhale the fragrance. The whole house would be pervaded by the odour, which was not at all unpleasant.

Although in later years coming downstairs in the morning was a great trial to Granny, she never wasted a minute. On her descent down the stairs, walking backwards with one hand on the bannister, her free hand would be employed dusting each stair, as she slowly made her way to the ground floor. And although Gran's younger sister looked after her in her later years, Granny made all the decisions.

Grandma: some of her ways

Granny always dressed smartly, and wore dresses of a darkish hue, but never black. She read the *Manchester Guardian*. She was always knitting or crocheting and made wonderful tablecloths with open work. All the family were kitted out in Granny's hand-knitted socks. She would start a sock in the morning, knit all day, retire to bed in the evening early, sitting up among the pillows because of her asthma, and would have that sock finished before she went to sleep. The tell-tale evidence in the morning of her nocturnal work would be well hidden (except for the finished sock) as all the little ends of wool would be stuffed in the seam of the flock mattress. She was so tidy. When we went to stay with her we played gin rummy. She didn't like to be beaten, so we generally let her win.

All provisions were delivered to the door. The greengrocer would bring round the cart packed with fresh vegetables, the milkman would bring the churn, and a jug in which to put the milk; the proprietor of the grocery store would personally call for the order each week. Going into Manchester happened only on high days and holidays, but if she went anywhere, Granny took a taxi.

One day, when my Granny was on one of these trips to the big city and my mother was very small, they saw a little girl sitting in the kerb, eating orange peel. She was crying. She said her name was Polly and that she belonged to no one. The outcome was that my Granny took the little girl back to her house, looked after and cared for her, giving her a home in return for light domestic duties. Later my mother had a family, and Polly came to live with us, in Surrey, where she died aged eighty.

Granny died in 1940, aged seventy-five years.

The Definitive Victorian Wife

Agnes Hogg (1854–1948)

Grandma was a very modest and placid homemaker.

My Grandmother was Agnes Hogg, née Pitt. She was born in March 1854 at Whitwell on the Isle of Wight.

She was a lady's maid *par excellence*, I would imagine, as she was sent to London for training. Back she came to the Isle of Wight where she was employed by a titled family, whose house still stands overlooking the sea. It is now a hotel.

On Boxing Day 1883 she was married to Edwin Hogg of Brightstone, on the island at All Saints parish church in Ryde. He was a master carpenter. Work was hard to find on the Island, and so my Grandparents moved to Southampton, on the mainland, where my Grandfather found employment.

Grandma was very modest and a placid homemaker. The 'Harvest Home' at the farm of my Grandfather's sister, who lived a few miles away, was the highlight of their year. Occasionally there were visits back to the island, mainly to see relatives.

Gran wore ankle-length black skirts, and a long black coat. Her blouses were always high-necked, and she wore black button boots. My Grandparents had two daughters. We always spent Christmas with them; sometimes they would come to us for a visit in Bournemouth.

Agnes Hogg

Gran walked everywhere, but when she stayed with her sister-in-law at the farm she travelled in a donkey cart. She often told me stories of how, returning home, she would trip over a cow, grazing in a field, in the dark, her light being a solitary lantern.

Grandma was bedridden for the last twenty years of her life. She died in January 1948 at Southampton, having outlived Grandpa who had died eight years previously. One of the first bombs to land in Southampton landed in my Grandma's garden but my Grandparents were unhurt.

The Scottish Matriarch

Ann Bonar (*c.*1860–1914)

Bedridden during her later years, she insisted that her bed be taken into the kitchen. She could then supervise and organise.

y Grandmother, Ann Lemon, married my Grandfather, Joseph Henderson Bonar, who was a master joiner, in 1884, at Auchenblas, Kincardine, Scotland.

My Grandmother was tiny, being well under five feet. She always wore black, with a band around her neck and a skull cap, both heavily encrusted with jet beads. Although my Grandfather was well over six feet and a very large man, Grandmother ruled him and the family of five children with a rod of iron. She was the local dressmaker. She attended Church of Scotland and all her married life lived in Peterculter, Aberdeen.

Although Grandmother was bedridden during her last years, she insisted that her bed be taken into the kitchen, where all our meals were cooked and eaten, so that she could supervise and organise, and still be the centre of attention. She lay there watching everything, and if something or someone displeased her would lash out with her stick. We tiny ones kept well out of her reach!

My Enigmatic Grandma

Eliza Ann Bobart (*c*.1850–?)

She married a soldier, and was promptly disowned by her well-to-do family.

My Grandmother needed a passport when she visited the Continent with her husband in 1877. Eliza Ann Bobart was a governess. She needed a passport to travel abroad with her employers. In 1877 the passport was signed by Edward Henry Stanley, Earl of Derby, Baron Stanley of Bickerstaffe, a Peer and a Baronet of England, a Member of Her Britannic Majesty's Most Honourable Privy Council, Her Majesty's Principal Secretary of State for Foreign Affairs, etc, etc. It reads:

> Request and require in the Name of Her Majesty, all those whom it may concern to allow Eliza A. Bobart (British Subject), travelling on the continent to pass freely without let or hindrance and to afford her every assistance and protection of which she may stand in need.
>
> Given at the Foreign Office, London, the 30 day of July 1877.

My mother never spoke about her mother or father in my hearing. Any conversation Mum was having with another grown-up ceased immediately I entered the room. 'Not in front of the children' was the order of the day in our household. It was only after my mother died, and we were forced to go through her papers, that I discovered that Grandma had come from a well-to-do family, and I gleaned some knowledge of her from our neighbour, who had been friendly with her.

The neighbour told me that against Gran's parents' wishes, Gran had married a soldier, the result being an abrupt and final 'cut off' from her family. There were two children from the marriage, a boy and a girl. As the result of my Grandfather's hard drinking, Grandma was forced to sell her two houses in Alma Road, Bournemouth. She took up residence with my parents. I never saw my Grandmother, as she died before I was born.

I was also told by a neighbour that Gran had been a very talented lady, who could draw well, and play and teach the piano. In fact, she kept a

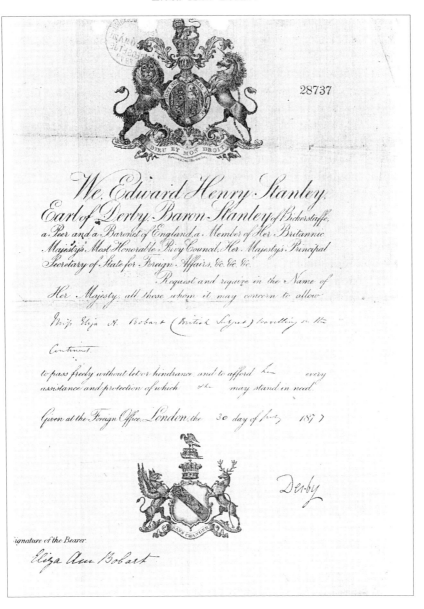

private school, possibly a 'dame school', hence the need for two houses side by side. There were many dame schools in Bournemouth at this time, around 1900.

Grandmother's passport shows that it was issued in her married name, my mother's maiden name being Bobart. So was Gran going on a honeymoon trip with her soldier husband in 1877? We will never know. Anyway, there is her passport for all to see. I was amazed, on visiting a local stately home, to see a passport belonging to a member of that family, framed, and hanging on the wall, exactly like Gran's! But Gran kept hers hidden.

What interesting and exciting tales Gran could have told to me, but if Mum had any information about Grandma, she kept it a secret from me.

So in my dreams, I ponder over those early days of Gran's. Did she come from the Dorset countryside to Bournemouth, seeking to supplement her income, now that she had been cut off from her family? Or did she come to Bournemouth seeking anonymity, like Mr d'Urberville, in Hardy's 'Tess'? Hardy called Bournemouth 'Sandbourne' in his novel. What was his vision of that town?

> Clare went up and down the winding way of this world in an old one, and could discern between the trees and against the stars the lofty roofs, chimneys, gazebos and towers of the numerous fanciful residences of which the place was composed. It was a city of detached mansions: a Mediterranean lounging place on the English Channel: and as seen now by night it seemed even more imposing than it was.
>
> The sea was near at hand, but not intrusive: it murmured, and he thought it was the pines: the pines murmured in precisely the same tones, and he thought they were the sea.

So wrote Thomas Hardy at the end of the nineteenth century. How well he knew and loved his Dorset landscape!

Sometimes it makes me sad that I do not share memories of my Grandparents when so many other families are only too pleased to tell their children about 'where they came from'.

My consolation is that where others have the hard facts, I can be allowed to dream . . .

Part Two

The Diaries of Mary Lett
1864 and 1865

Tear off the calendar
Of this month past,
And all its weeks, that are
Flown, to be cast
To oblivion fast.

'The Months' Calendar'
Thomas Hardy

A Discovery

 solicitor's office was being redecorated. During this time, a brown paper bag was discovered behind a cupboard, which revealed a pocket book dated 1813 marked 'Stoke', two diaries dated 1864 and 1865, and a crumpled piece of embroidered linen dated 1869 marked 'Scampston'. Accompanying these artefacts was this information written on a scrap of paper:

> Mary Parrott, wife of Charles Parrott, of the Brick House, Stoke; Mother of Mary Parrott, who married Joseph Lett, of Rushock, in 1839.

The pocket book belonged to Mary Parrott. The diaries belonged to her daughter, Mary Lett, whose name is inscribed on the front piece.

The beautifully preserved sampler was worked in 1869 by Mary's daughter, Annie Lett, whose name is embroidered on it.

Because all these items were left in the dark cupboard, they are just as they were when handed in for safe keeping a century and a half ago.

Because this book is about Grandmothers and their Granddaughters, we have included photographs and details of these artefacts. They add another dimension to our path of discovery into the lives of Victorian women.

We can learn quite a lot about a person from their diary although the two diaries in question, dated 1864 and 1865, being so small, left little room for much information – just the facts of the day to day existence of a farmer's wife in the north of England. As was the custom of the day, the writer always referred to her husband as 'Mr Lett'.

How can we sum up Mary Lett's life?

We know that she married at twenty in 1839, because her mother had written it for us. 'Mary Parrott, who married Joseph Lett, of Rushock, in 1839.'

Annie Lett was twelve when she embroidered the sampler in 1869. This would make Mary Lett about fifty at this time, possibly making her Grandmother to Annie. There is one reference to Annie in her diary of 1864:

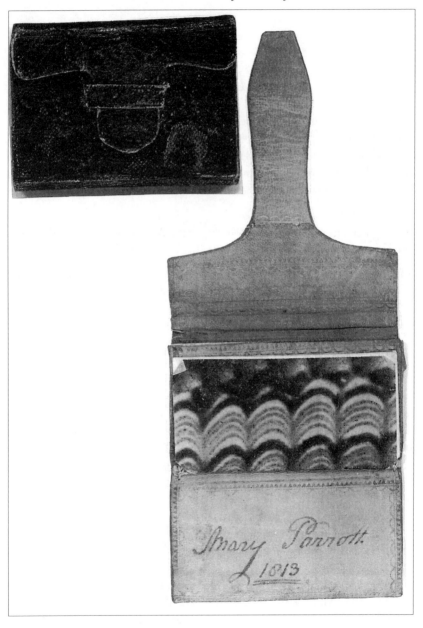

Mary Parrott's pocket book. It contained six pages, with marked end papers

A Discovery

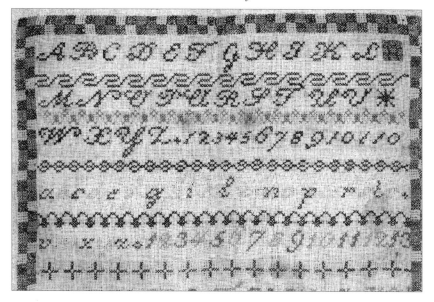

Annie Lett's sampler, 1869

Wednesday March 16th 1864
Mr Hicks here to tea. Mr Lett, Sarah, Anne and I went to church in the evening.

In 1864, Anne, or Annie, would have been seven years old.

We can also learn from Annie Lett's sampler, which was beautifully and carefully embroidered, using cross stitch only. There is not a spare space – all the open linen cloth has been employed. The sampler is worked using upper and lower case letters and the alphabet is in its entirety. Each time the alphabet has been worked, a different border divides the work, and it is as neat on the reverse as on the face side.

The sampler is worked on open linen with single stranded red and blue coloured thread. It is assumed that Annie worked it at school where, at twelve years old, she was probably in her last year.

We can also assume that she was well loved, for the sampler to be regarded as an heirloom. Perhaps the sampler was recognised as a 'leaving certificate' of the day, and although not many families still retain them, it is safe to say all girls, whatever their status, worked one at some time.

A few extracts
from Mary Lett's diary

1864

Feb 1st Mr Lett with us all day. Mrs Bedford gave her notice.

   8th Mr Fox took tea with us, at night.

   9th Shrove Tuesday. Washing day. Jane here.

   12th Mr Hughes came after tea.

   15th Killed two pigs for ourselves. Mr Lord from Norton came after tea.

   16th Made pork pies. Mr Lett at home all day.

   17th Mr Goodman took tea with us.

   23rd Washing day. Harriet and Jane went to tea.

   25th I wrote to Mr John Lett.

   27th Jane poorly with shingles.

Mar 7th Anne the servant returned home.

   16th Mr Lett, Sarah, Anne and I went to church in evening.

   25th Good Friday. Went to church in morning.

May 20th Sheep shearing finished.

June 9th All of us at home. Mr Lett reading 'good works'.

   13th Mr and Mrs Hicks came after tea and spent the evening.

   14th Threshing wheat.

   29th Went to look for a servant girl.

Sept 3rd Doctor's Bill 7s. 6d.

   9th Harvest Supper.

   15th Mr Lett went into Worcestershire.

   17th Heard from Mr Lett.

A few extracts from Mary Lett's diary

The diaries of Mary Lett, née Parrott

   24th Mr Lett returned.

Oct 18th Colonel and Ma came to look at the house.

   20th I made elderberry wine.

Nov 8th Mr Lett went hunting.

1865

Jan 2nd Mrs Lett, Miriam, Harriet and I dined at Cumberson.

   3rd Went with Harriet to Bedales Minster. Lunch at Cumberson.

   6th Mr Lawley's party. Harriet and I returned to Stowe.

   10th Mrs Hardoe came. G. Hill, Mrs Clerk, Mrs Emole and I took tea.

   11th John took me to Hagley. I took a very bad cold.

   12th Harriet returned from Dudley. Came to Hagley. Harriet and I went home.

   13th Mrs Wooldudge sent us to the Woodcow. They had a coursing party there.

   16th Harriet and I spent the day at the Rectory.

   17th Mr Lett came to Mr Hill in evening.

   18th We dine at the Hills.

   19th Mr and Mrs Lett, my husband's parents, and I took tea with Mrs Codmoney.

   24th Mr Lett and I dined at Yew Tree.

   25th We dined at Mr Arnphletts.

   27th Went to Marston and stayed there all Saturday.

   31st At home all day.

Mar 1st Papa and John returned from Leeds.

   18th Mary and I went to Malton with Mr Lett.

   20th Mr Lett and Fred at Pickering. I went to Scampston Hall and took tea.

   21st Killed two pigs.

   29th Mr Lett and Fred returned from Leeds. We killed a pig. The first day of warm weather.

A few extracts from Mary Lett's diary

April 3rd Mrs Lord confined on the 2nd inst. I went to see her in the evening of the 3rd.

11th Brewed our first ale at Scampston. Killed two pigs.

14th All at church in the morning. At home in the evening.

15th Fred and Mrs Lett at Malton. I went to Mr Lovell's after tea.

19th Mr Lett at home all day with a sore throat.

20th All at home all day. After tea I went to call upon Mrs Hicks. She was not at home.

21st Mr Schofield. Bought a horse called Nelson.

May 4th Washing day.

24th Mr Lett and John went to Norton in new dog cart. A heavy shower of rain at night.

27th Mr Lett, Harriet, and myself at Malton. A fine day. Fred rode the grey mare.

Jun 5th Went to the Hall in morning. Fishing in afternoon.

23rd Mr and Mrs Lett, Mrs Pardoe, my husband and Harriet went to Whitby.

Aug 19th Mr Lett and I went to Malton. I lost my satchel there.

Sep 13th Papa and John at Doncaster to see the St Leger. Returned same evening.

Oct 5th A very fine morning. Dipping lambs. Mr Lett rather poorly.

6th Mr Lett went to Mr Newton's to tea. Very poorly after he returned. A very bad night.

7th Dr Allanson came to see Mr Lett. He is better in the afternoon.

11th All set fair at Malton.

13th Mary drove me to call upon Mrs Dunkley who was confined the Sunday before.

30th Mr Lett and myself went to see Dr Allanson, Mr Lett being unwell.

31st Mr Lett better.

Nov 2nd Doctor Allanson spent the evening with us.

21st Mrs Kill called. The Earl of Dudley's wedding day.

22nd Mr and Mrs Lovell called after tea. We were very busy cleaning.

26th Mr Lett and I went to Willington Races. Took tea with Mrs Packer.

Dec 5th Elizabeth Normington entered upon her service.

6th Killed a pig. Mr Lett and I took tea at Mowgate with Mr and Mrs Topham.

8th I was making pork pies. Henry Crumpton dined with us.

19th Papa and myself went to Scarborough. I dined at Mr Hills.

Bibliography

Thomas Hardy: *Poems of Thomas Hardy*. A new selection by T.R.M. Creighton, (Macmillan Press Ltd, 1974).

Thomas Hardy: *Tess of the d'Urbervilles*. (Macmillan and Co. Ltd, 1966).

Hampshire Directory 1857. By kind permission of Hampshire Record Office.

Appendix

Names and birthdates of Grandmothers

Bobart, Elizabeth	1850
Brocklesby, Isabella	1874
Bonar, Ann	1860 *circa*
Bedford, Charlotte	1888
Bestow, Charlotte	1874
Blandford, Eliza	1880
Botto, Emily Sarah	1873
Carter, Mary Ann	1862
Coker, Annie Maud	1883
Cross, Mary Ann	1846
Davis, Bessie Marguerite	1872
Frith, Martha	1880 *circa*
Hardiman, Catherine	1883
Harrison, Mary	1860 *circa*
Head, Emily	1870 *circa*
Hogg, Agnes	1854
Howlett, Louisa Jane	1860
Jones, Gwendoline	1850
Jordan, Margaret	1865
Knox, Emma	1880
Lemon, Emily	1878
Lett, Mary	1840 *circa*
Lindsay, Helena	1877 *circa*
Parkin, Kate	1870 *circa*
Passills, Elizabeth	1863
Powell, Elizabeth	1878
Saunders, Fanny	1850 *circa*
Smith, Constance	1874
Stark, Hannah Mary	1872

Surridge, Mary Augusta	1855
Voisey, Eliza	1880
Warr, Elizabeth	1860 *circa*
West, Lilian Emily	1882
Wilson, Patience	1862
Wright, Agnes	1840 *circa*
Wright, Mrs	1860 *circa*